Alternatives to hierarchies

International series on the quality of working life

Vol. I

Alternatives to hierarchies

Ph. G. Herbst
Work Research Institutes, Oslo

Martinus Nijhoff Social Sciences Division
Leiden 1976

ISBN 90 207 0632 2

Printed by Mennen, Asten, the Netherlands.

Preface

Giving on occasions a talk on the subject of this book, one of the queries raised was, 'surely, what you mean are flat hierarchies'. This, I think, gives an indication of how difficult it can be to conceive of organizations which do not have a hierarchical structure. A rather similar response was obtained when, in the 1950's, an account was given to a manager of the British Coal Board of an autonomous composite team of more than 40 miners, who had taken over complete responsibility for a three-shift cycle, and divided the income obtained among themselves. His comment was that this could not possibly work. The new mode of work organization which had been evolved by the miners in several pits in the Durham coal fields was, at the time, well ahead of the prevailing concepts and philosophy of both management and the Trade Union. It did not help matters very much that the detailed accounts were presented in an academic and scientific form (Trist et al., 1963; Herbst, 1962). I think that we felt that all the backing of systematic research and data analysis would be needed to present the case for modes of organization, which deviated from conventional practice.

However, something was learned from this experience. When at the beginning of the 1960's the Norwegian Work Democratization Project was started, a number of demonstration sites were set up which people could look at, and which could function as centers for diffusion. There was no immediate success with this as far as Norwegian industry was concerned; however, a rapid diffusion occurred some years later in Sweden.

Action research is essentially a long term collaborative learning process of those who are involved in a process of organizational change. It was results of this type, where theoretical expectation and practical experience diverged, which in recent years have led to reflections on and a reappraisal of the socio-technical approach which was developed in the course of project work, of the strategies of organizational change which have been utilised, of the role of the expert, and of the conditions for diffusion.

In their recently revised account of the early Norwegian field sites, Emery and Thorsrud (1977) note that what we had initially taken to be a machine theory of organization turns out to be a particular form of a general theory of bureaucracy. It would seem that it might be quite difficult to say anything very new about bureaucracies. However, utilizing the socio-technical approach makes it possible to identify the design principles of bureaucratic hierarchies in a simple form, and once this is done it becomes possible to identify the basic characteristics of a whole range of alternative non-hierarchical forms of organization. Apart from the autonomous composite group, this includes matrix and network organizations. Each of these will be appropriate for specific types of tasks and environmental conditions, and the last two appear to provide possible modes for large scale organization.

Part II looks in more detail at the perennial twin threats to society. The threat of disintegration and chaos and the attempt to impose some form of totalitarian order. The approach developed in this work is to look for and to identify in each case the basic assumptions which, if they are accepted as being true, generate a particular form of organizational logic. In the last chapter, the question of the nature and origin of the basic structures in terms of which we organise our world, leads to a basic reformulation of the foundations of logic itself.

This book is an outcome of a long term collaborative effort of a network of colleagues which began to be formed about 25 years ago. At that time Fred Emery was a senior lecturer at the Dept. of Psychology of the University of Melbourne, and the author was a student member of the research staff. About that time, Einar Thorsrud during a stay in England had become aquainted with Eric Trist and A. T. M. Wilson, the then chairman of the Tavistock Institute. During the 1950's Fred Emery and the author worked at different times with Eric Trist at the Tavistock Institute on the coal mining studies and the development of socio-technical analysis. In 1959, I spent about 6 months in a hut in the hills outside Trondheim to complete a monograph on 'Autonomous Group Functioning'. In the course of a visit to Einar Thorsrud, at that time director of the Institute for Industrial Social Research, I accepted an offer to work at the Institute, and some years later Fred Emery and Eric Trist from the Tavistock Institute collaborated with the Institute in Trondheim on the Norwegian Industrial Democracy Project. About that time, an informal European group was established, which included among others Hans van Beinum and Mauk Mulder in Holland, and subsequently Louis Davis contributed on problems of socio-technical design. It is in part a review of our own organizational experience which helped in identifying some of the characteristics of a network group.

My thanks to our secretary May Hoelsaeter for her kindness and help. For permission to reproduce material that has already appeared in print, thanks are due to the following: The editor of *Acta Sociologica* in respect of Chapter 3, and the editor of *Social Science Information* in respect of Chapter 7.

Work Research Institutes
Oslo, 1975

Contents

Part I.

Alternatives to bureaucratic hierarchies

Part 1
Alternative
to bureaucratic hierarchies

1. Strategies in the democratization of work organizations

The development of alternative forms of organization can be looked at in terms of different strategies which have been used to transform existing organizations. In the process of change the basic assumptions and characteristics of bureaucratic hierarchic types of organizations have become more clearly visible. At the same time, and gradually, the basic structural elements of alternative types of organizations could be investigated and their emergent properties studied.

1.1. The Bottom-Up Approach

Since the start of the Norwegian Industrial Democracy Project this has been the most widely used approach. The argument is as follows. The hierarchical organization is based on the segmented tasks at the bottom of the pyramid. The coordination of the tasks of individual workers and decision making is split off and allocated to successively higher levels of the organization. If the bottom layer of the pyramid is transformed then this should lead to the restructuring of the successively higher levels. A start in this case is made by establishing the conditions for the formation of autonomous groups on the shop floor to take responsibility for a total task which may be extended to include boundary functions such as material supply and quality control. In so far then as the foreman is no longer needed in his traditional role he may need to be given a higher level role, which then requires changes at the next level, and so on. What is expected to result is an upward cascading process.

This approach requires from the start support from the top of the organization and the trade union. The unintended outcome at the next stage is frequently found to be a squeeze of middle management (Fig. 1.1). The same outcome was in the Norwegian experiments found to occur in the trade union. Support was received from the top of the union and from shop stewards, but just as for middle management so also for the middle layer of the union, the changes were inconsistent with the established techniques of production control and wage negotiation.

While this approach is well worthwhile, it tends to be contained around the boundary of the foreman level. Also, in so far as middle management is forced into a defensive position, it becomes more difficult at the next stage to look at and work through requisite changes at the middle management level.

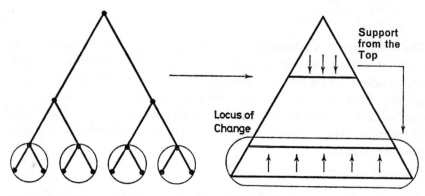

Fig. 1.1. Establishment of autonomous groups at the bottom level.

1.2. The Top-Down Approach

Reviewing the experience at this stage, the Tavistock Institute suggested the possibility of starting at the top to obtain an agreed on policy, and then obtaining policy commitment at successively lower levels by a downward cascading process of conferences. This approach was implemented at Shell UK refineries from 1965 onwards. Specific implementations resulted at some refineries in the direction of increasing the level and range of responsibility of operators, and some years later one manager went ahead to carry out a full scale project. The results indicate that widespread involvement was obtained at both the top and at the management level at several sites.

There appear to be several reasons why difficulties were encountered in maintaining the implementation process. Among these

1. In the process of downward cascading, motivational commitment is created at the top and middle management level but not to the same extent at the bottom level.

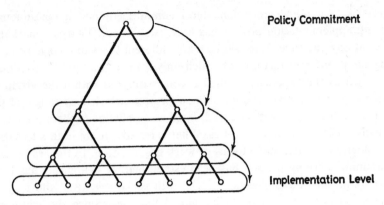

Fig. 1.2. Downward cascading policy commitment.

2. When the implementation process does not gain impetus, the initial motivation may become dissipated.

My impression of this particular case is that once a *general* commitment was obtained it became a source of conflict to allow *some* managers to go ahead with implementation while other managers were unable, or not in an equally good position, to do so. Since not everybody could go ahead with implementation at the same time and with the same chance of success, the managers caught in a possible highly visible prestige conflict, found that a slow and careful approach in which no manager would go ahead too fast on his own, but which allowed each one to take some, if only token implementation steps, would be in their joint long term interest. While in other cases the process has run into the encapsulation of specific individual change sites, here the process in the implementation phase took the form of a general diffuseness.

1.3. The Center-Down Approach

The squeeze of middle management in the first approach has as one of its major sources the role adopted by the researchers in the early experiments, who took over both the control and responsibility for the organisational change process. In the course of the diffusion of the initial results to Sweden, responsibility for the change process was taken over by middle management. This was possible since many of the firms concerned have a sufficient number of professionals and also some social scientists on their staff. Of particular interest is 'Volvo', where a long term commitment and a continuously evolving implementation process has been established. What is remarkable is that at any one time there will be many different types of change projects going on at different factories of which only some attract public attention, and which as the experience gained becomes diffused within the group of factories, lead to the starting off of new projects which may range all the way from job enlargement on a traditional assembly line to the more recent successive redesign of new factories. What is tested out are both alternative technologies and alternative forms of work organization. In this way a self-maintaining learning process has been established. A major role has been taken by production engineers together with social scientists who may be attached to headquarters or to individual factories. Since the major responsibility for the success and failure does not lie with the factory manager, and also since change projects can be started at a site without necessarily attracting immediate attention, even within other parts of the firm, personal prestige conflicts and encapsulation processes have not been a major problem.

The problem which has emerged is an increasing inconsistency between the ulitization of traditional production control techniques, in this case a highly sophisticated MTM system, which forms part of the national agreement with the trade unions, and the steps taken to increase the level and range of responsibility of the workers on the shop floor. While at Volvo there are indications of the existence of two cultures within management, there has been no evident split and conflict within management. At the shop floor, however, the contradiction between MTM work measurement and the actual task and functioning of work groups has become a source of a potentially chronic conflict and grievances. There is a possibility that at the next stage, steps may be taken to deal with the problem that has emerged.

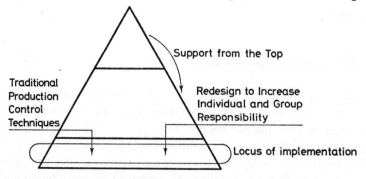

Fig. 1.3. Inconsistency between traditional management techniques and implementations to increase individual and group responsibility in the center-down approach.

1.4. Horizontal Project Groups

A relevant and potentially convergent approach was developed by NASA in the US. In response to the growing awareness of the fact that significant tasks and problems cut across hierarchical levels, temporary project groups were established. Once their task was completed, project team members would again return to their position in the hierarchy. One of the problems encountered is the development of dual and potentially inconsistent loyalties.

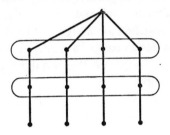

Fig. 1.4. Horizontal project groups.

The aim in this case was to find a way of increasing the viability and flexibility of a bureaucratic hierarchical type of organization, rather than an approach to transform the basic structure of the organization. However, potentially, this approach could be used as a way of transforming the organization itself. If the hierarchical organization is abandoned as the basic structure, we would then have a set of organizational units each with a specific function but each able to become a temporary part of, and function within, different types of task groups, depending on the nature of the problem encountered. In this case transition towards a matrix type organization would become possible.[1]

1.5. Vertical Slices (Participant Design)

Reviewing the experience gained so far in the beginning of the 70's there was a developing recognition among those actively involved in democrati-

1. In the Hydro experiment a horizontal project group was established which included a member of the Institute staff. At Hunsfos a more vertical type of project group was established with the initiative of the management. This group functioned more independently and utilized the Institute as consultant. (Emery and Thorsrud, 1976).

zation projects that the approaches which had been developed could come to be used as a new set of management techniques. There appeared to be a possibility that in the course of diffusion there might develop a new profession of socio-technical experts, who would in the traditional top-down way design systems for others. A democratization of work organization is scarcely possible without the direct involvement of those concerned in both the design and the implementation of new organizational forms.

Working at this time in Australia, Fred Emery formulated the vertical slice approach. In this case a temporary project group composed of members from the workers, foreman level and up the line of command, comes together to evaluate the existing job design and work organization and then jointly formulates a new design based on creating conditions for work group autonomy. Similar slice groups are then established for each shop floor unit resulting in a sweeping slice.

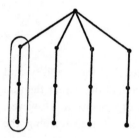

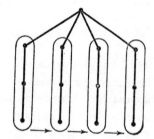

Fig. 1 5a. Vertical slice group.   *Fig. 1.5b.* Sweeping slice.

1.6. The Center-Out Approach

In the approaches so far the locus of implementation of change projects has been the bottom layer of the hierarchy. In industry this is the personnel directly involved in production work. The utilization of different types of project groups within the firm in the change process suggests the possibility of related changes within the middle management level.

In the case of other organizations such as shipping and schools the basic tasks are not in the same way found to be allocated to the lowest level of the hierarchy. Here, the possibility of transforming the central core of the organization can more easily provide the conditions for changing the organizational structure as a whole.

In a school project, the locus of change has been the development of cooperative relationship between teachers in the design and implementation of total student projects. This immediately changes the learning situation for students who can in small teams take responsibility for a larger task. Working upwards the next step would need to be an increased responsibility for teachers as a team to take over responsibility for the school as a whole. An increased level and range of responsibility of teachers would then provide more room for pupils to be given increased responsibility and participation in task relevant decisions.

There are indications that the center-out approach is particularly appropriate to change projects in ship organization. On board ships the basic tasks are carried out by junior officers. Starting with an extension of the competence range of ship officers, providing overlapping skills in navigational and engineering task, a change project in the direction of a matrix organization for ship officers has been established. At present the training of the subordinate crew is based on training on both deck and machine. Provided unskilled work at this level can be reduced, the function of the crew could then be raised to that of officer trainees. The transformation of the central core of the hierarchical structure appears to provide in cases of this type the best way for changing the organization as a whole.

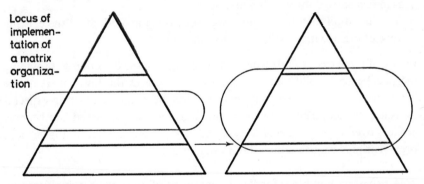

Locos of implementation of a matrix organization

Fig. 1.6. Center-Out Approach in the case where the basic tasks of the organization in its traditional form are carried out at the middle range of the hierarchy.

1.7. A review of stepwise procedures

All the change strategies discussed so far have two characteristics in common. They are based on
1. a stepwise procedure, and

2. based on the utilization of external or internal experts or special techniques.

The stepwise procedure to be successful has to take the form of a continuous
organizational learning process. For this to occur at least two conditions
have to be fulfilled.

1. The first step taken should, to the extent possible, avoid creating countervailing and defensive pressures specifically from middle management to
encapsulate the change process and thus stop the transformation and learning
process. The vertical slice approach is an attempt to involve middle management, workers and trade union representatives from the start. In the
center-out approach, which is appropriate in some cases, the initial locus
of implementation is the middle range level of the hierarchy. If the process
runs to a stop at the first stage then this may have several reasons:

a. Middle management may at the start find itself encirculated by top
   management, the workers and external change agents.
b. The change agents and the members of the organization may believe
   that what is involved is a one-step change towards a new type of organization which can be submitted to before and after studies, when what
   is in fact carried through is a first opening.
c. The intention may be to find a way for saving and adapting the existing
   type of organization rather than to transform it.

In any of these cases, while worth while changes in the direction of providing
increased responsibility and autonomy for those at the lower level of the
hierarchy can be achieved, internal inconsistencies and conflicting expectations are created. The problem is that what has been achieved can become
eroded over time, or become nullified by subsequent technological and
organizational changes along traditional lines.

2. A necessary condition for the development of an organizational learning
process is that the locus of initiative is developed and lies within the organization itself. It is here, where the external change agent has a major responsibility. If his main concern is that of demonstrating his competence as an
expert he will, without necessarily being aware of this, achieve the opposite
and block the development of a change process. Adopting a technocratic
role, or perhaps more correctly sociocratic role himself, his aims will be
contradicted by his practice. If on the other hand he adopts an ostensive

non-directive role, this will not be very helpful either. The problem for the external change agent is to enter into a relationship where joint learning becomes possible. His task may or perhaps should not be the actual implementation of any new system, but that of contributing to the discovery and development of appropriate starting conditions for a process which can go on its own way.

1.8. Critical One-Step Transformations

The most successful cases of establishment of autonomous work organizations are those where external change agents either from outside the organization or from middle management were least involved. Autonomy, freedom and responsibility can not be imposed. The critical factor in the most successful cases is that the workers concerned had or took the opportunity to design, implement, evaluate and develop further their new form of organization either with the consent or after contractual negotiation with local management and with the active support of the local trade union representatives. What happened in each case had the characteristics of a culture change.

The fundamental problem is that the new forms of organization towards which one seeks to move are both in their structure and mode of functioning totally different from the conventional forms of organization. If the point of departure is a highly bureaucratic hierarchic organization, then it may be necessary to utilize a stepwise procedure. Sooner or later, however, it will be necessary to go through a critical one-step transformation out of and over to the new form of organization. In this phase, when moving out into the unknown, no longer securely anchored in the familiar, and before one has arrived at and begun to orient oneself within the new context, it will be essential that the participants in the organizational change process have achieved agreement on the direction in which they wish to move and have achieved sufficient trust towards one another.

Cases such as the autonomous work organization established by the miners in Durham county and the Hommelvik experiment have a number of characteristics in common.

1. In each case the groups concerned took responsibility for the production of a total product. In the coal mines a contract was negotiated for a three monthly period based on the price per ton of coal produced. In the Hommel-

vik experiment the workers took responsibility for the manufacture of panel ovens as a total product. Given this, and depending on the size of the task, a single or a joint set of groups was established which took over the responsibility for production planning and work allocation. Where a set of groups was established, rotation across groups provided cohesion within the larger system.

2. In each of the cases the sites concerned were not tightly imbedded in a bureaucratic hierarchical structure, but were at some distance from central headquarters. The typical staff of a coal mine is a manager, a secretary, some safety inspectors and a few foremen. The foremen in the traditional form of mining organization have a production control task which they can scarcely cope with. Being relieved of their supervisory role they have more important tasks to attend to in the way of providing technical planning and support. Similarly in Hommelvik the local staff consisted of a manager, a secretary, and in this case the foreman's role could be absorbed into the production team. There was in these cases no immediate need to work through the middle management and specialist problem. While this was an advantage in the short run it was also a weakness in the long run as far as survival possibilities were concerned. Each of the innovations remained vulnerable to the imposition of individual piece rate systems based on centralized wage negotiations or the imposition of traditional rationalization techniques based on MTM systems. Where they survived they did so as somewhat exotic and overlooked plants within an environment in which they had become benignly encapsulated.

Utilizing the stepwise approach in industry, and having at this stage demonstrated the viability of autonomous types of work organization within a wide range of industrial undertakings and in different countries and cultural settings, the next step is to work through the problem of the management and the specialist production and planning staff level. This at the same time implies the need to work through the problem of production control and planning technologies.

There are at least three possibilities:

1. Transformation of production management from a control to a support function.
2. Disconnection and where appropriate absorption of relevant production management functions into viable autonomous production units.

3. Going beyond the establishment of autonomous units within existing hierarchical organisations to the development of alternative organizations of the firm as a whole in the direction of a matrix type organization.

In the projects within the Norwegian shipping industry, the implementation of more autonomous types of ship organizations has led to the understanding that a correlated reorganization of headquarter staff becomes necessary. At the stage where middle management goes beyond establishing organizational changes for its subordinate level, to the point, where the need is recognized to transform its own organization as well, a critical step will have been taken. In this case also a change in the role of external change agents and researchers will be facilitated in so far as these in their work take a *de facto* substitute or auxiliary middle management role. If steps in this direction can be successfully implemented then both the bottom-up and center-down approaches will become validated.

At the same time, the possible utilization of the one-step approach, where an opportunity exists, should not be overlooked. The indications are that this approach is both more efficient and also can considerably reduce the costs involved in protracted organizational change. The one-step cases fall into two types. In one of the coal mining cases, the pit was threatened with closure, due to uneconomic working. Under these conditions representatives of the workers proposed the composite and autonomous work organization and in the course of a number of days and nights, worked out a formal contract with the local manager. In the Hommelvik case the small, quite primitive subsidiary factory in a country community functioned at the time as a site for small risk operations. In both cases then the risks involved in a more total change were minimal.

There are a number of cases in recent years were workers have made successful bids to take over the management of factories which were on the point of going bankrupt. Their bids were in many cases backed by concrete proposals which would make it possible to carry out production more effectively and economically if the management was taken over by them. The take-over of a firm by the workers may not by itself solve any problems if the traditional organization is maintained. Even the factories which were established in the Israeli kibbutz were originally established with a basically conventional organization design, and it is only more recently that steps have been proposed for alternative types of organization.

One of the more recent examples of a new emergent model in the form of a one-step change is the case of the Meriden motor cycle factory cooperative in England. Here the contractual agreement reached is for the workers to take over the management of the factory leaving buying and marketing of the product to the parent company. In the new type of organization suggested the significant change made is the abandonment of job demarcation making it possible for any man to take over any task which he is capable of doing as the need arises.

While it is too early to judge the success of this innovation, the organizational design evolved and suggested by the workers at this plant points in a direction of a model which may in time turn out to be both economically feasible and consistent with the aims of the democratization of work organizations.

Each of the approaches discussed have been described in their simple 'pure' form. Project groups whether at the top, middle or bottom level, in the form of slice groups or in the way of downward cascading have each been used either individually or in some form of combination to facilitate the bottom-up approach. In long term change projects, consecutive changes in the approach utilized are part of the process of organizational learning. It should be noted that whichever of the stepwise approaches is chosen to begin with, both countervailing forces and inconsistent operational systems may be created which at the next stage determine the opportunity and alternatives provided for subsequent steps.

In the choice of possible organizational structures set up for the purpose of implementing a change process what needs to be taken into consideration is:

1. The extent to which the structure set up to initiate and facilitate changes some place else, provides at the same time the conditions for requisite changes within the higher organizational levels and in the role of external change agents.
2. The extent to which the initiative for the change process together with the responsibility for design, implementation and evaluation becomes located and is maintained within the organizational unit, or set of organizational units, engaged in the change process.

A more detailed account of the cases referred to can be found in the following:

Approach	
Bottom-Up	K. Rice (1958) E. Thorsrud and F. E. Emery (1969) and F. E. Emery and E. Thorsrud (1976) P. Engelstad (1970) J. Roggema and E. Thorsrud (1974)
Top-Down	P. Hill (1971)
Center-Down	P. G. Herbst (1975)
Horizontal Project Groups	Kingdon, R. D. (1973)
Vertical Slice	F. E. Emery and M. Emery (1974)
Center-Out	J. F. Blichfeldt (1973) J. Roggema and N. K. Hammarstrøm (1975)
One-Step	E. Trist et al. (1963) P. G. Herbst (1962) J. Gulowsen (1971) F. E. Emery and Thorsrud (1976)

2. The logic of bureaucratic hierarchical design

2.1. Introduction

Some of the basic characteristics of bureaucratic organizations are becoming more clearly visible in retrospect as we move away from them to explore and implement other forms of organization. For the problem before was that it was difficult to see an alternative. Seeing is a rather curious thing for the alternatives have existed all the time, so if we were not able to see them then this is because they did not fit our logic and our theory of what ought to exist.

Nature makes no distinction between flowers and weeds. We do, and once we make the distinction we can build our logic on this and be very rational about it. But sometimes we have to look and to ask whether what we thought was a weed was not 'really' a flower. When we do this, our logic may go to pieces. And perhaps there is not so much harm in this as we think. In fact, it may turn out to be a good thing.

The bureaucratic model developed in Europe to:

1. Replace forms of organizations based on arbitrary authoritarianism and nepotism.
2. It provided a way for organizing large number of people in a uniform and standardized way which was easy to control and administrate from the top.
3. It was consistent with the value of equality both internally and towards those whom the organization was meant to serve, and with the value of logical rationality. At the same time it provided the basis for modern industry and large scale administration and it was consistent with a mechanistic scientific world model based on the concept of uniform, replaceable parts i.e. the idea that organizations can be built and made to function in the same way as a machine.

It is fairly obvious that people and organizations which function in this way are replaceable by machines. However, this is not helpful until it is seen that human beings and organizations can function in a different way and also relate themselves to machines in a different way.

The bureaucratic system can become inhuman to the extent that it becomes the predominant system for organizing human activities, and when adherence to its rationality becomes a self-legitimising aim and value in itself. While adherence to rules, programmes and computer logic represents an attempt to overcome the problem of arbitrary authoritarianism it does not solve the problem of human responsibility.

When Hannah Arendt in the discussion of the Eichmann trial talks about the banality of evil what I think she points to is that inhumanity within the modern civilized world derives from the willingness of man to sacrifice others and sometimes himself to his logic and thus an inability to see that logic as such has no value but people have. If this is the case, then it will not help to appeal to people to be more humane if this is something which they feel compelled to sacrifice for the achievement of a 'higher' aim. In order to find the way out, one needs to go back to discover and confront the assumptions which have created the logic in which people can get themselves caught and which, seeing no choice, and often with the best of intentions, they feel impelled to impose on others. When it is found that the basic assumptions which generate a logical system have no reality value then the chain of logic with which people bind themselves and others will be found to be insubstantial and to see, that that which binds us becomes unsubstantial when we are no longer attached to it, is the way of discovering one's inherent freedom.

2.2. The logic of bureaucratic organization

In order to understand the characteristics of an organization we need to know the assumption it makes about the nature of its task.

The basic assumption which generates a bureaucratic hierarchical structure is that:

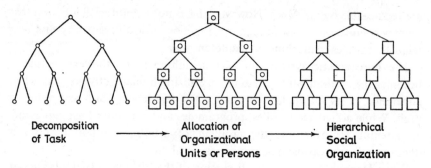

Decomposition   Allocation of   Hierarchical
of Task   Organizational   Social
                       Units or Persons   Organization

Figure 2.1.

Assumption I
The organizational task can be decomposed successively into smaller and smaller independent bits.

Assumption II
Each unit or person should be allocated exclusively to a single task element.

As a result, what is obtained is a hierarchical structure (Fig. 1). The organization will as a consequence have the following characteristics.

Consequence 1
A *single* structure of relationships between units.

Consequence 2
A *uniform* type of relationship. Units and persons are linked exclusively by a superior-subordinate relationship.

Consequence 3
Every unit and person has, in terms of its or his functions, a single clearly demarcated boundary.

Consequence 4
Since the only relationship that is given between units and persons is a superior-subordinate relationship and if both decision making and task performance is required, then decisions about task performance are made by the superior level for the subordinate level which in turn makes decisions for the task performance of the next subordinate level. As a result

Consequence 5
The principle adhered to within the organization is that of splitting decision making from task performance.

Consequence 6
In terms of the theory the top level is left with decision making but no necessary task performance, while the bottom level is engaged in task performance but may be left with no decision making.[1]

The organization arrived at in this way is not yet fully bureaucratic since it does not exclude the possibility that individual units and individuals below the top level may have some areas of discretion and autonomy. These possible free spaces are abolished in two ways by:

1. Provision of rules and programmes which regulate task performance without the need for constant personal and direct supervision.
2. The superior is held accountable for the performance of his subordinate and will tend to invade his remaining possible areas of discretion either personally or by technical work control means. And also he himself is subject to invasion of his possible areas of discretion by his superior.

Sub-division of tasks and detailed performance specification appear to be to some extent independent characteristics.

The bureaucratic model is a good theory in so far as it provides a simple logically consistent model, and this is also the reason for its potential inadequacy. If implemented the organization may not be able to function and survive without the development of informal practices and relationships. Where this happens, it is possible to spend large amounts of time in organizational planning and change projects which operate in terms of the theory, but may not relate to the way the organization actually functions or may need to function.

At the same time, one cannot overlook that there are conditions, especially in the field of public administration, where bureaucratic organizations function well. These cases would be interesting to identify and study. The analysis so far indicates that relevant conditions for this are:

1. Consequences 1-3 can each be treated as assumptions. What is shown is that these assumptions are related to one another in a logically consistent way, so that, given at least a pair of these, the others become derivable.

1. That the task can be decomposed into independent parts.
2. Both the nature and requirements for task performance are stable over fairly long periods of time.
3. Sufficient areas of discretion and responsible autonomy with respect to task performance exist at all levels so that even the lowest level provides the opportunity for the performance of a relatively autonomous professional role.

At the present time these conditions are decreasingly met since on the hand both the nature of tasks and requirements for task performance are no longer stable over long periods of time, and routine tasks which can be programmed can be computerized and automated.

The present search for alternative forms of organization which started in industry has at least two major reasons. The first is that by taking the bureaucratic model to its rationalized conclusion, industrial tasks were split into the smallest possible bits, and task performance was to the extent possible completely specified or dictated by the machine. Since the human conditions of work for those at the bottom of the hierarchy were recognized to have become increasingly intolerable, the possibilities for alternate types of work organization have been explored. At the same time it was possible to see that a transformation of the lowest level of the pyramid might provide a way for requisite changes of the upper levels of the hierarchy. The concern here is predominantly with finding ways for inproving the quality of working life which requires fundamental change in the organization of work in the direction of debureaucratization. This in turn made it necessary to examine alternative ways in which tasks can be structured and organized.

The second reason is that there are increasing indication that the nature of the task which faces organization is such that hierarchical bureaucratic organizations can no longer cope with them. The bureaucratic model is based on the principle of vertical control. The nature of the task is increasingly that of needing to cope with the management of a complex ecological type network of horizontal dependencies. (Figure 2.2). Moreover the nature of relevant tasks and their interdependency can change quite rapidly and unpredictably over time.

The problem then is that at time of increasing environmental turbulence as pointed out by Emery (1974), the bureaucratic organization is mismatched with and unable to come to grips with its problems, and by making inappropriate responses may contribute both to the external and to its internal turbulence. When this happens the traditional problems of bureaucratic

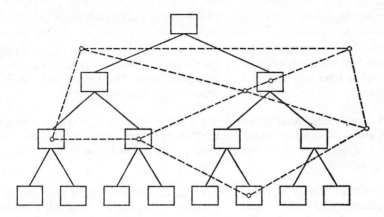

Fig. 2.2. Mis-match between vertical control and a changing network of horizontal task dependencies.

organizations become considerably aggravated. The inability of the organization to cope with its task then becomes a major additional source of human dissatisfaction which may take the form of apathy, withdrawal or revolt. At this stage the problem of improving the quality of working life goes well beyond that of improving the job satisfaction of organizational members with their task, since the actual nature of the task which people need to be concerned with and the way in which it can be managed has become the problem.

The following table summarizes the assumptions of the bureaucratic model. Actual organization may deviate from this model and none of the basic and derived assumptions will hold for non-bureaucratic organizations.

Bureaucratic Model	Non-Bureaucratic Organizations
1. The task is taken to be divisible into successively smaller and independent task elements.	Task elements may in some cases be independent but are generally linked in a network of dependencies. The pattern and nature of dependencies may shift over time.
2. A single hierarchical structure exists in terms of which units and individuals are related to one another.	There are many types of structure generating relationships and those which are most directly task related can rapidly shift over time.
3. A uniform type of superior-subordinate relationship which excludes relationships between units and individuals on the same level.	There is no uniform type of relationship. In the relationship between units and individuals one or other may take a leadership role. In some tasks there may be joint activity and decisions. Where task units are independent, autonomous decisions will be possible. However where task interdependence exists, autonomous decisions will be expected to be consistent with the maintenance of directive correlations with the activities of other units or individuals with whom task dependence exists.
4. Each unit has a single boundary which is clearly defined.	Segmentation and demarcation of boundaries are not the principle on which the organization is based. There may be several types of boundaries or none, and minimal or no pre-specification. Boundaries were these appear may be emergents of the organizational process and competence range, in relation to the characteristics of the task structure, geography and communication. Units and individuals may have a primary task and responsibility together with a wider range of competence so that boundaries may not be clearly demarcated and can change over time.
5. Boundaries separate units and individuals.	Boundaries may be overlapping, or they may contain units or individuals working together on a task in which case the boundary may again disappear at a later stage.

2.3. Task structure and the process of organizational design

In the following we shall discuss each of the assumptions which stem from the basic task structure and to consider how each of the assumptions can and need to be modified. One incidental result is that a good deal of social science and organization theory turns out to be based on, or consistent with the specific properties of bureaucratic models. This is perhaps not surprising since in both cases the search has been for a model which is both simple and logically consistent.

Also researchers found that large scale organizations were predominantly of this type, or considered the model as an ideal type.

2.3.1. Assumption 1.
A task can nearly always be decomposed into smaller and smaller independent bits

If this is the case, then it becomes quite difficult to accept that alternatives to hierarchical and bureaucratic organizations are rational or feasible or to conceive of such changes as more than modifications of isolated bits at the bottom of the hierarchy.

By concentrating on the Tayloristic consequences for job design which are logical consequences of this task model and which impinge specifically on the bottom level of the hierarchy, we may be paying insufficient attention to the fact that similar types of dysfunctional consequences are found at higher levels in the form of boundary disputes, power struggles and difficulties if not inability to finding ways of cooperative problem solution.

It would appear that a basic source both of inefficiency, alienation and turbulence lies in the mismatch between organizations built on the pattern of vertical control and tasks which require management of a network of horizontal dependencies. Under these conditions where the allocation of tasks and responsibilities does not match task requirements the outcome may be passive retreat into protective indifference at the bottom level and active involvement in chronic personal and departmental power conflicts at higher levels. Here again by concentrating on work alienation at the lowest level we may tend to overlook that task estrangement although manifesting itself in a different form can be at least as much a problem at the management levels. The implications for participant design, in a way in which both workers and management could be concordantly engaged would be to start off with the requirement of working towards a matching of the organizational design with a network of predominantly horizontal dependencies both within the organizational unit and the relationships to and within the environment.

In this case it may become easier to see that

1. The organizational design generated will not necessarily take the form of a pyramid.
2. The one person – one task, one department – one function model can and needs to be departed from in order to handle changing task loads and shifting patterns of interdependence.
3. It will be found that there is no way in which a set of units separated by 'water right' boundaries can be made consistent with the requirements of horizontal dependencies, specifically when the type and pattern of dependencies may change quite rapidly. The 'ideal' of split off bounded units is in fact the logical outcome of the bureaucratic task structure. This may not mean that the ideal of bounded systems needs to be abandoned but that boundaries may be partially overlapping and that different units may not have exclusive ownership of specific functions.
4. Given a design based on multi-skilled individuals or multi-functional departments, then the matrix type organization which is generated will not have a single rigid structure. In fact the organization which results has no one single structure, but provides a multiplicity of potential structures appropriate to shifting task and interdependence requirements and thus raises the question of local autonomous control together with the need for directive correlation between different parts of the organization.[1]
5. The type of organization arrived at along these lines should generally satisfy basic job design criteria or make it possible to find suitable adjustments.

The discussion up to this point shows that once we depart from the bureaucratic model then a number of assumptions which have provided the basis for traditional organization design have to be abandoned, together with a number of often implicit principles which have been taken for granted in organization theory. In the following a number of these assumptions which are generally unrecognized logical consequences of the bureaucratic task model will be considered.

1. The concept of directive correlation was formulated by Sommerhoff (1950) and introduced in the social sciences by F. E. Emery (1967 b).

2.3.2. Assumption 2.
An organization has a single structure which can be put down on a piece of paper

The pictures which are made of organizations generally consist of squares or sometimes circles linked by lines. Rather like the stick and ball models of a molecule. We may of course be doing some injustice to molecular models which are often of considerable complexity and which do have the merit of corresponding closely to the actual molecular structure, which is rarely, if at all, the case in organizational models. However, the basic assumption is the same, namely, that organizations can be put together and constructed by taking components and linking them together. The difference however is that while molecules can take a vast variety of forms, and thus develop a variety of properties, organizations practically irrespective of what their task is to be are constructed to take the simplest model given by the assumption which generate a hierarchy. This may be reasonably feasible if the task has a bureaucratic structure. However one should not overlook that if this type of organization is judged to be the only feasible way to organize human activities then tasks will be shaped and tailored to fit the organization. Thus by establishing a bureaucratic structure for education what goes on within the organization may end up by not constituting education in much more than a formal sense.

If as is generally the case the task can not be split into more and more independent bits, then the implemented design becomes a kind of monstrosity which could scarcely operate and survive in practice unless people either informally or in other ways went beyond the formal structure to find ways of making it work. This however has a number of consequences.

1. There may be scarcely any correspondence between the actual functioning of the organization and the theory, so that the organization whether a corporation or a psychiatric hospital may acquire schizoid characteristics in a rather literal sense.
2. When organization design, planning and reorganization are carried out in terms of the 'ideal' model, the organization becomes chronically unmanageable, and relief may be sought by replacing managers or engaging in constant technical and administrative reorganization. In this process,
3. The task of the organization recedes into the background and becomes a boundary condition for maintaining the bureaucratic structure, and

4. as internal turbulence or costs increase there may be a strong temptation to adapt simplistic methods of centralized computer management, teaching machines and other techniques for direct rigid organizational and behaviour control without being able to consider the human and social costs involved.

It can be quite difficult to drop the assumption that organizations can or should as a general rule be designed and imposed as a single rigid and pre-specified structure.

It will be shown in a later section that even simple organizations evolved by the participants themselves have a far greater sophistication. Instead of a single structure in terms of which roles and responsibilities are rigidly defined, they are multistructured and instead of a fixed allocation, relationships are found to shift rapidly in response to variations of task load, and task requirements.

Organizations of this type are not predesigned but evolve in a process of organizational learning given a set of critical boundary conditions which may be arrived at by negotiation or exist by common agreement, and within which required autonomous responsibility can be maintained.

2.3.3. Assumption 3.
Organizations are of a uniform type

In part the problem here is of mistaking the label for reality. Thus an authoritarian group may be thought of as one where everything is decided by the leader and a democratic group as one where everything is done and decided together. This becomes a problem chiefly if organization design and implementation are taken to be the achievement of an ideal system.

I would think that this is a problem chiefly for those for whom the real world is that which is given by theories, while that which is given in fact can be eliminated or interpreted to fit the theory or, alternatively can be shaped and made to fit the theory. To loose such a theory, which may represent all that is of value, and also that which constitutes the reality within which one exists, can then be quite threatening.

Some years ago when I was engaged in a family study I came across the case of one family where husband and wife did and decided about most things together. This family was among those with the highest amount of tension and conflict. It appears that what they were trying to do, was to implement a democratic family organization and in so doing were not able to accept that where appropriate one or other could make a decision, nor were they willing to provide sufficient autonomy in the way of permitting each other to engage and decide about some activities themselves.

While there were families who were dominated by either husband or wife there was none where unilateral decisions affecting others was more than a relatively high or predominant pattern. An attempt by any one partner to make anything approaching all decisions would have been quite unlikely to allow the family to survive. Equally an attempt to develop a wholly autonomic type of family where each has his own activities about which he decides for himself would not have worked, since to maintain the existence of the family, at least some social and economic activities have to be carried out and decided jointly.

It would appear that an attempt to develop a uniform type of organization will be made whenever the members of an organization are unable to trust one another, that is, where they are unable to develop a way of cooperation where they can trust that each individually has the competence and willingness to act in a way which takes the needs of others into account and which will be in the common interest.

Thus if any one partner in the family pre-empts the making of decisions to the maximum extent, or if both as far as possible seek to act and decide for themselves, a condition of mutual trust will not exist. However this will also be the case if the principle of making joint decisions on most matters is adopted.

Autonomous groups and matrix type of organizations do not have a prespecified and uniform structure. Depending on the nature of the task at any time, members of a group may work together, split into pairs, and individual may at some point work on their own. Nor is it necessary for decisions on work allocations to be made by group decision if group members individually are committed to a cooperative group task. What is needed in this case is that team members all have access to information on the state of the task, the task which other are engaged in, and an either implicit, or where necessary explicit understanding of a joint strategy which may as a result of learning change over time.

In organizations of this type, a uniform and rigid organizational structure does not exist. Instead members have the freedom needed to develop relationships of mutual support and are able to adapt work allocation and work relationships to shifting task requirements. Going one step further, an organizational network has no specific internal structure nor does it require that members either work or make joint decisions except where under appropriate conditions they see the need to do so.

2.3.4. Assumption 4.
Organizational units have a single exclusive boundary

There are at least four separable assumptions involved.

1. Every organization has a boundary which can be clearly demarcated.
2. The boundary has to be fixed in position and is an essential property of the system.
3. Organizations have a single boundary.
4. Organizational boundaries are exclusive, i.e. The boundary separates systems from one another.

What we encounter here are not simply what may be taken to be necessary characteristics of organizations. If we take the field of knowledge as a whole, then we split this up into humanities and science. Science is split up into chemistry, physics, biology etc. Chemistry is again split up into different subjects, and even if bridging disciplines are established such as physical chemistry, these tend to become specialised subjects. In this way the field of knowledge can acquire the characteristics of a bureaucratic hierarchy within which each unit has a single exclusive boundary.

In classical physics atoms were conceived to be like billiard balls. In grammar, sentences are decomposed into atom-like elements linked by a hierarchic structure. The same method of decomposition into smaller and smaller units, each with a single exclusive boundary, is followed in production engineering.

The dominant mode of organization design is based on the same type of assumptions. The best way of showing that these are not necessary assumptions, is by studying the nature and mode of functioning of non-hierarchical organizations.

3. Non-hierarchical organizations

Processes of social change often move from a given state to its opposite or to its converse. Moving in any of these directions the transformations achieved remain contained within the logic of the given.

Moving out of an authoritarian structure which has become discredited, obsolescent or inefficient a transition may occur to a converse authoritarian form. Alternatively, if an authoritarian structure becomes simply eroded, as happened in the Victorian middle class structure of parent-child relationship, then a transition may go to its opposite, a laissez-faire relationship. From here a transition may occur at the next stage to an authoritarian form in new institutional settings such as para-military youth movements. Changes of this type are shifts within an essentially one-dimensional conception of society. It is more difficult to find and achieve a fourth alternative which is neither authoritarian nor laissez-faire and which lies outside the logic which generates this type of process cycle. (Fig. 3.1).

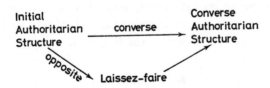

Fig. 3.1. The process of social change is locked within the logic which generates the organizational structure.

In much the same way, transition from a pattern of competitive individualism within an academic community may take the form of establishing the opposite, which is making group decisions on all issues.

In the case of bureaucratic hierarchical organizations, an attempt to move out of this system may be perceived as going in the direction of the opposite, that is, a chaotic unstructured state. Alternatively, transition from say a centralized to a decentralized system produces the converse without necessarily changing the basic mode of operation of the organization.

There has been a view that a hierarchical organization is the only possible form of organization. This would be true, if each of the component parts are restricted to a specialized function. In this case a single structure of hierarchical levels is generated to coordinate the functioning of the specialized parts.

The alternative argument has been that since each element is part of a larger whole, which is again part of a larger whole, and so on, a pattern of hierarchical domination is inevitable. This assumes that part-whole relationships is the only way in which elements can be related to one another.

Here again then, the process of social change can become locked within and unable to go beyond the inherent organizational logic. The steps required to find a way out, are to

1. identify the basic assumptions which generate the organizational logic,
2. search for an alternative set of assumptions,
3. derive the characteristics of alternative types of organizations.

The basic assumption which generates bureaucratic hierarchical structures is that each member is restricted to a single specialized task. As a result, a single structure of hierarchical linking relationships is established within which the functioning of each level is controlled by the next higher level.

If the one man-one task principle is abandoned, then the requirement for a hierarchical organization disappears, and what results are organizations which instead of having a single rigid structure of relationships have the capacity for multistructured functioning (Fig. 3.2).

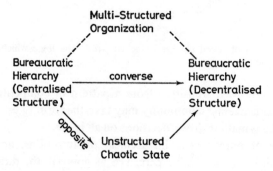

Fig. 3.2. Identification of a fourth alternative.

The first case of an alternative type of organization which was studied in some detail is the composite autonomous group. This is based on the principle that each member is able to carry out all, or at least most tasks. More recently it was discovered that if the principle is adopted that each member has a specialist function, but at the same time an overlapping competence with other members, then what is generated is a matrix organization. Figure 3.3 shows the type of organization generated by each of these design principles.

Fig. 3.3. Alternative types of task allocation which lead to different types of organizational structures.

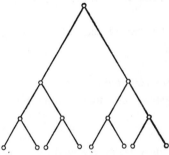

One man – one task, generates a single structure of hierarchical levels.

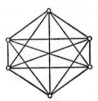

Each man – all tasks, provides the conditions for a composite autonomous group, and allows any structure of work relationships to be utilised.

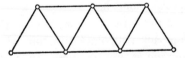

Each man has an overlapping competence with other members, provides the conditions for a matrix organization. In the above case, each man is capable of carrying out two to four tasks. This type of organization has a basic structure, but at the same time allows a variety of possible work relationships to be utilized.

The study of non-hierarchical organizations of this type shows that these have the capacity for functioning by way of directive correlation of the activities of members who may be working independently or in smaller subsets. That is, although members may work independently for shorter or longer periods, the work of each supports and facilitates the work of others in the direction of the achievements of a joint aim.[1] This makes it possible to identify the operating principle of a network in which members may be geographically dispersed and have no form of direct control over one another.

In the following we shall discuss the characteristics of composite autonomous, matrix and network organizations, first at the level of small groups, and then consider the feasibility of these types of organizations at the level of larger social units.

The common characteristics of each of the different types of non-hierarchical organizations are

1. the capacity for multi-structured functioning,
2. the capacity for achieving and maintaining directive correlation of on-going activities.

Each of the non-hierarchical types of organization points to the possibility for developing organizational relationships which not only permit but also support the individual autonomous development of members, going beyond the choice between the Scylla of competitive individualism and the Charybdis of collectivistic and authoritarian solutions, thus avoiding the sacrifice of the individual to the over-riding needs and demands of a social system.

Historically, the first non-hierarchical type of organization which was discovered and described in some detail is:

1. The *composite autonomous group*. Within this type of group all members are capable of carrying out all or at least most tasks. The members of the group being equipotential, none has a special leadership function. The special characteristics of this type of organization is that it has no specific structure but can adopt any temporary structure which is judged by the members to be appropriate at any one time. Thus, there is no necessary requirement for all members to work together on any task or to make group decisions. They may at any one time each work individually or in subsets.

---

1. The concept of directive correlation was formulated by Sommerhoff (1950). Its relevance to the study of social systems was pointed out by F. E. Emery (1967).

However, the requirement in this case is that the activities of individual subsets of the group remain directively correlated towards the joint achievement of a specified aim. The requirement that all members are able to carry out all tasks has as a consequence that the required competence range for the total task will need to be within a feasible range. The size of the group is generally relatively small. However, there are examples of linked sets of autonomous groups which can operate as a unit of up to around forty persons.

2. In a *matrix group* each member has a specialist function but each has an overlapping competence with some other group members. In this case there is a structural constraint. At the same time a large variety of alternative structures can be generated and utilised depending on task requirements. The special characteristics of the matrix group is that, as far as the design principle is concerned, there is no necessary limit to the size of the group. However, there is no practical experience so far which might indicate the approximate limits to a viable group size. The design principles for this type of organization were initially theoretically formulated, and it is only quite recently that an implementation has been carried out on board a ship. This does not mean that matrix groups have not existed in the past without having been recognized. A recent study has shown that some of the characteristics of a matrix organization have been traditionally evolved in at least some banking branches.

3. A *network group* can be described as the converse of an autonomous group. The members of a network are normally dispersed individually or in small subsets. It is only infrequently that they come together as a joint group in a work session and for direct communication. In an autonomous group on the other hand, the members normally work in close association with one another and network type properties emerge in the work situation only temporarily and for shorter periods, whenever the group splits into smaller subsets in carrying out its task.

The basic characteristics of a network is the maintenance of long term directive correlations, mutually facilitating the achievement of a jointly recognized aim. The project of this type of organization is typically to find ways of going beyond the established given. As an organization it provides the maximum autonomy of individual members consistent with, and under some conditions optimally suitable for the achievement of a joint aim.

There are several reasons why organizations of this type tend to remain relatively unrecognized for long periods. Taking the case of a network of scientists as an example then:

1. Communications may be in the available literature but its significance may initially only be visible and actively responded to by relatively few others.
2. The aim may to begin with only be quite vaguely specifiable and possible means of implementation may to begin with be quite tentative and unclear to the network members themselves. The joint task and commitment of network members becomes that of working towards the clarification both of the aim and means of implementation.
3. A web of directive correlation is scarcely ever visible from the outside and may also to the participants become recognizable in its structure only in retrospect. It is not simply a matter of information flowing more easily within the network.

The type of process which occurs is that the contribution of member *A* may be recognized as an innovative step by member *B*, who may be able to take this further in his own work. This again may help *A* to see further implications. In this way a cumulative process within the network may lead to a new approach to a problem which is a joint product of the group. At the same time, approaches which show themselves to be inadequate can be rapidly modified or abandoned. The absence of individual status striving by individual members is a critical factor in being able to abandon or modify unproductive approaches. In this way the primary function of a network is the development and maintenance of a joint learning process, and its productivity depends on the actual or evolving complementary skills of its members. Both in the nature of its task, its mode of organization and its process of functioning, a network is possibly as far removed from a bureaucratic hierarchical organization as it is possible to get.

Although network groups may maintain their existence over some decades, they are in principle temporary systems. As such, members will normally maintain their role in more conventional institutional settings. In this case the linkage between different institutions may become a correlated function, which at the next stage points in the direction of a network organization in which the nodes are institutions. A network group, as its task becomes completed, that is as its approach becomes converted into a new established given, may become institutionalized as some kind of professional society, or the members may disband and move towards new fields.

Each of the types of organization discussed, have existed for some time, however, they have generally been either unrecognized or exceptional. Known actual cases at this time, whether discovered as naturally evolved forms or achieved by design implementation, are on a small scale. A study of cases of this type was essential to gradually developing an understanding both of the hasic design principle and the mode of functioning of organizations of this type. Table 3.1 gives a tentative overview of the characteristics of non-hierarchical organizations at the group size level. One of the basic

Table 3.1. Types of group organization.

	Bureaucratic hierarchical	Composite autonomous	Matrix	Network
Task structure	Product (P) procedures (π) and input state (I) are given by specification π (I)$\rightarrow$ P or assumed to be reducible to this form in terms of given norms and rules	Product is specified. Input states are specifiable but procedures are not, or a requisite choice exists ? (I)$\rightarrow$ P	There may be a variety of products. ? (I)$\rightarrow$ P or ? (?)$\rightarrow$ P Procedures and possibly input requirements are not specified.	Neither initial nor outcome state are specified in operational terms ? (?)$\rightarrow$? The task is to achieve a more specifiable task structure
Task competence range of members	One man – one specialized task	Each man – all tasks	Each man has a specialised task together with overlapping competence with other members	Overlapping compentence range of members
Organizational structure	A single specified structure of relationships	Can adopt any type of temporary structure depending on recognized task requirements.	A basic structure is given by the pattern of overlapping competencies but within this a variety of structures may be adopted.	Sets of members may and generally do engage in joint project work for shorter or longer periods. The structure is given by the web of directive correlations

	Bureaucratic hierarchical	Composite autonomous	Matrix	Network
Basic principle of organization	Parallel and independent activity of contiguous members. Regulated by specified activity programs and normative rules.	Mutual facilitation of contiguous members in direct interaction with one another. Joined and shared responsibility. Short term directive correlation when members work in smaller subsets.	Intermediate between composite group and network. Members work predominantly in smaller subsets and the pattern of all working together on a task is less frequently adopted.	Long term directive correlation of dispersed members. Selective interdependence.
Feasible size	No apparent limitation to the subordination of parts.	Sets of autonomous groups linked by rotation of members are possible. The possible use of this type of organization for larger scale units needs to be further investigated.	In principle there is no limit to the size of a matrix, however, the problem of viability has not yet been investigated. At the next level a matrix in which organizational units are components appears to be possible.	Network groups are limited in size. A network of networks appears to be possible. The main utilization of this type of organization lies in the development and maintenance of directive correlations of organizations involved in a long term change process.
Environmental suitability	The assumption is that the environment including human beings both can and should be converted to and maintained in a highly	While means – end relationships may remain basically predictable, operational conditions may be subject to marked varia-	The conditions may be such that a number of aims needs to be achieved in a coordinated way. At the same time a shift of aims can	In their original form network groups were established to tackle problems outside the established given. At present their relevance

Bureaucratic hierarchical	Composite autonomous	Matrix	Network
predictable form.	tions. At the same time autonomous groups have a capacity for both technical and organizational learning.	lie within or not too far beyond the adaptability range without requiring basic change of the organisational form. The matrix organisation provides in this case a balance between structural constraints and flexibility	lies in respect to mildly turbulent environments. Their stabilizing structure lies in the fabric of directive correlations. Matrix organisations are appropriate for production tasks. Network organisations are appropriate when a number of different organisations become involved in a relatively continuous and long term change process. Their basic characteristic is that the research function becomes incorporated and dispersed within the organization. It is at this stage that the traditional role of academic and research institutes with exclusive property rights to the research function is no longer appropriate.

differences between bureaucratic hierarchical and non-hierarchical forms of organization will be seen to lie in the fact that bureaucratic hierarchical organizations are based on the principle of a single rigid structure, while each non-hierarchical form of organization has the capacity for multi-structured functioning.

The problem at present is that of investigating the relevance and feasibility of the design principles for larger social units. There are at least two ways of proceeding:

1. If a change of scale occurs due to growth, then just as it is possible to develop larger bureaucratic hierarchical organizations with organizations of the same type as components, so it may be possible to, say, develop a network of networks.
   Alternatively:
2. The constituents of a matrix or network instead of being individuals, may be organizational units of different types.

There is insufficient experience so far with the possible utilization of autonomous groups as building blocks for larger units. There appear to be two possible problems:

1. The requirement that members are capable of carrying out all or most tasks restricts the size of individual units.
2. Autonomous type groups have for the most part been implemented within the structure of existing hierarchical type organizations, specifically in bottom-up change strategies, and thus built at least temporarily into an at least partially inconsistent context.

The approach which has been found specifically appropriate for large scale units is the network organization. This type of approach was in fact utilized from the beginning in the Norwegian Work Democratization project. To see its significance what is needed is a figure-ground reversal.

Organizational networks may in much the same way as project groups be utilized to implement changes somewhere else. In this case they function as adaptations of a fundamentally bureaucratic structure. Their mode of functioning as a non-hierarchical organization is quite different.

An example is the type of organization which has evolved in a project concerned with working towards a new form of organization on merchant ships, which initially was concerned with the development of an autonomous type group for the subordinate crew and more recently developing a matrix group of officers. A change of this type, requires, as it proceeds, a change in headquarter organization, a change in maritime schools which involves the Ministry of Education, changes in certification and regulation, changes in trade union structure and functioning, in the process and direction of technological architectual design, and changes also in the role of the researchers involved.

The implementation process, which involves changes in the mode of functioning of each of the constituent organizations and also in their relationships to one another, is almost precisely the same as that described previously for the little network group. The project is to go beyond the established given. The aim to be achieved finally cannot initially be specified in detail. The initial time horizon may be 10-15 years. The project is such, that no organization by itself can go ahead very far on its own, since it is linked to the other organizations involved by interdependence and complimentarity relationships which become manifest in the change process. The major difference as compared to the informal network group is, that while interdependence relationships of the latter are a result of selective interdependence, the initial structure of interdependence relationships is given by the nature and scope of the change process.

Given in the present case an initial joint commitment of the organizations concerned for initial exploratory steps in the direction for change accepted, a representative committee was formed which then constitutes the formal core of an evolving network group. Taking to begin with exploratory steps for changing the organization on board project ships, provisional facilities for additional education of officers for a matrix organization was required. With the agreement to go further, a new structure for maritime education has been established which affects both career paths and certification requirements. What becomes visible now, is that while before the captain had to be recruited via the deck department, he can now be recruited from any member of the matrix group. To implement an extension of the new form of organization, what needs to be explored at the next stage are requisite changes in the organization at head office and the development of new types of relationships between head office and ships. At the same time, ship personnel has been involved in the design of new living quarters which have been implemented providing saloons and restaurants for the total crew, and a raise and equalization of cabin facilities, thus removing one of the traditional supports of the earlier segmented, hierarchical status structure. The extension of the number of project ships has at the same time led to a diffusion network between different shipping companies. At a later stage, a need for the change of the trade unions, which are at present based on the traditional work roles may become recognized.

What is meant by a figure-ground reversal in the present case is that the initial object of change becomes at the next stage a means for the transformation of the larger social system. Within this process, each of the participant organizations is able to change itself adaptively in relationship to other participant organizations. Within the organizational network, the process of change moves along the lines of a gradually evolving fabric of directive correlations. Each implementation step becomes subject to evaluation, and after each step, new steps forward may become visible and subject to exploration. In this way a continuous learning process is developed and maintained within which theories and guiding hypothesis become evolved and modified in a constant confrontation with the empirical results obtained. What is found here, is a possible alternative to traditional ways of achieving social change which, whatever the ostensive and often idealistic aims, may, by their mode of implementation maintain the established given and at worst add momentum to the extension and preservation of bureaucratic or authoritarian social orders.

An extension of a matrix structure to the next higher level becomes possible if we have a set of organizations, each with a specialist task but with some overlapping competence which can link in smaller and shifting subsets in carrying out their tasks. It would appear that within a matrix organization, autonomous type groups will have a more appropriate context, given that they are able at this stage to take an active participant role within a larger organizational context.

4. Reflections on the work democratization project: the process of diffusion

In the early 60's we were concerned with testing whether and to what extent autonomous types of work organization which had been shown to be feasible in the British coal mining industry, were feasible in manufacturing industry. At the same time we expected that changes in this direction would:

1. provide a way towards the democratization of working life at the shop floor level
2. improve the quality of working life
3. create organizations capable of functioning in non-stable environments
4. be consistent with the increasing level of education of the population as a whole.

Towards the end of the 60's a number of successful demonstration experiments had been established in Norwegian key industries. At this stage the problems encountered were:

1. An encapsulation of field sites. Diffusion did not necessarily occur to other departments in the same firm, nor to other firms in the same industries.

2. Apart from minor modifications of the technology, existing designs were taken as given. While significant progress has recently been made in finding technological alternatives in line production (Volvo, Saab), unsolved problems remain in mechanical manufacturing where a variety of products are routed through the factory.

3. Key concepts used in launching a project can become a problem at a later stage. The aim of the project was perceived as the introduction of more or less self-regulating groups. It has been more difficult to get across that the changes involved are towards organizational forms which are qualitatively different with respect to several dimensions. At the same time, the project has

often been perceived as a transition from one system of work to a different one which could then be evaluated once the project was finished. What is assumed here is that the process which comes into being is something temporary and dispensible and what is of lasting value is the new system structure which has been evolved. What is needed is a figure-ground reversal. The new characteristics of the process is the goal. The structures arrived at are temporary. They may have brought us nearer in the direction intended, and once achieved they provide a vantage point for seeing where one has come to, the nature of the new landscape and the next steps to go. The more enduring characteristics at this stage lie in the quality of the developmental process. This becomes clearer to people who have become engaged in change projects of this type. Once people have learned to walk, also the theory is dispensible. On the other hand even if one has a good theory about it, this does not by itself help anyone in learning how to walk, although it may be helpful in acquiring a reputation as an expert.

4. It is only fairly recently that we found that a distinction has to be made between the type of strategy required to establish demonstration experiments and the type of strategy during the diffusion stage. The indications are that the type of strategy which may be optimal for setting up demonstration experiments may have negative consequences at the diffusion stage. There may be a number of reasons for this.
a. Those involved in the experiment may develop the culture of an elite and feel that they are rather special and superior. If those in the immediate environment grant that what has occured in the experimental unit is very special then the implication is that it has no general validity. In this case both sides may contribute to the encapsulation process although for different reasons. The immediate environment may then become practically vaccinated against the change process which has now become contained. If one then looks for a diffusion effect, this may well have occured, but not necessarily where one looks for it.
b. For the pioneers involved in the demonstration experiment the pay off in the case of success is considerable, while the loss in the case of failure is minimal. For those who follow after and are asked to use the demonstration experiment as an ideal model, the pay off in case of success is minimal (after all it has been done before) while the loss in the case of failure will be considerable.
c. In setting up demonstration experiments, researchers establish a special commitment and responsibility for the field site which is necessary, but

tend to aquire also a *de facto* personal ownership of the field site. The risk at this stage is that of entering into a collusive dependence relationship which is well known in theory from the psychoanalytic literature but difficult to avoid getting caught in in practice. What happens at this stage is that a special relationship is set up to a few selected sites, and this relationship is by its nature exclusive. The result may then be:

i. field sites become or are maintained dependent on the researcher

ii. since this type of relationship can only be extended to a few field sites, the researcher contributes to the encapsulation of field sites.

Looking back there appear to be three stages in an action research project each of which requires a distinctive strategy together with specific role and institutional relationships. There are indications that at each stage both the type of commitment and competence developed together with the type of competence and role expectations generated in the relevant environment may make it difficult to make the transition to the next stage.

The first stage shows some of the essential characteristics of academic research. The methods used are descriptive and analytic field studies. Economic support is generally based on time limited funds from a public research foundation. The difference from pure academic research lies in the fact that from the start, field work has the characteristics of a more or less wide ranging search process. The aim is to identify possible emerging innovative trends, and to diagnose existing situations which are known to be problematical in order to generate alternative possible directions for development.

The problem encountered at this stage is that even if individual researchers are prepared to go on to the next stage, that is an active involvement in a social change program, the institutional structure and public image created during the research oriented phase may make it difficult to create the environmental links required for the transition.

During the 50's the Tavistock institute developed its distinctive competence chiefly within the first stage of action research. Funding was based on consultancy relationships with client organizations and some time limited research funds. On the local scene it had developed in the direction of an encapsulated elite institution. Diffusion of ideas was minimal within Great Britain, but appeared to proceed more easily in Europe and Overseas. There was an active discussion towards the end of the 50's between those with a more local and those with a more cosmopolitan orientation, that is between those who felt that active project engagement should be maintained within

Great Britain and those who felt that cooperative project work should be established with institutes abroad to make use of emerging diffusion possibilities.

During the 60's the Trondheim and later the Work Research Institute in Oslo were able to develop their distinctive competence chiefly in the second action research stage, that of setting up demonstration experiments and working through long term socio-technical changes with a number of selected firms. A critical factor which made this possible was that a totally different linkage was established to the relevant environment. From the start relationships were established with the employers' organization, trade union, and the society for engineers, and members of the board of the Trondheim institute were able to establish contact and obtain support from members of the ministry, government and key industrialists. This made it possible to obtain long term national funding of the project with the continued support of all the major political parties in Norway. Being independent of specified time limited research grants made it easier for institute members to avoid defining themselves or be defined as academic researchers. At the same time the difficulties involved in dependence on consultancy contracts with individual firms could be avoided. It was possible, and this more easily in the more recently started shipping and education project, to circumvent the long term traps involved in accepting either the role of a traditional researcher or that of a consultant and to define a new role as action research as a cooperative venture in a relationship where neither party had any direct financial dependence or benefits from the other.

The stage of demonstration experiments was completed by the end of the 60's. In the preceeding I have discussed some of the conditions which led to encapsulation at the end of this stage. This appears to be related to the type of strategy utilized, specifically in so far as it led to the formation of a small elite in-group of firms with whom direct project participation of researchers could be maintained. The situation which was interpreted as one of stagnation, was one where a massive diffusion began to occur across the borders, specifically to Sweden and at present there are indications that a similar process may be on the way in the US. It is noteworthy that this diffusion has occured typically without the utilization of external research institutions. Firms have been able to utilize their internal staff. As a consequence, middle management instead of being put into a squeeze, and thus often into an oppositional position are able to take instead an initiating project leadership role. In fact they have now taken over a good deal of the researcher's role, which they were not able to do as long as the firm looks to an external research institute for *de facto* project leadership.[1]

This raises the problem of the role of research institutes in the third stage when the diffusion process is on the way. At this stage the relationship between researchers and organizations has to change.

1. At the diffusion stage direct participation of researchers in the organizational change process is no longer feasible nor acceptable. The researcher will then no longer have a horse to ride on. This is clearly not a negative sign, since no large scale diffusion process can get on the way until organizations see the need and judge themselves capable to go ahead on their own.

2. While up to the stage of establishing demonstration experiments the researcher has an active initiating role, the problems encountered at the diffusion stage can generally not be solved by trying to push the process along. What is required is the identification of obstacles encountered, and finding ways of overcoming them or sometimes circumventing them. The obstructions encountered are often structures which were established to supply the supporting conditions for the previous organizational form, and in this case the problem becomes that of creating new types of supporting conditions. The obstructions may at any one time lie within or outside the organizational unit and it is in the latter case that a larger network of participants will be required. Inevitably the obstacles encountered will at times lie outside the range of speciality fields within which we have most experience and where we feel most at home. They may lie in the field of technology, economics or law, or sometimes come up in locations where no scientific discipline has sought to establish territorial rights. (We have for instance been involved in participant planning of the location and layout of living quarters on board ships as these were found to be critical factors in the process of changing the established status structure). It is especially in cases, rarely found outside action research, where the process takes us across established disciplines or where none exist, that both the special opportunities and also need is encountered for a new development in theory and method.[2]

---

1. The contributions which members of the institute have made to the diffusion process in Sweden and at present in the US were made with the expectation that this would support the diffusion process in Norway.
2. We are perhaps for the time being nomads in the scientific world. However it is of course also possible to claim belongingness to a specific territory on the formal grounds of academic descent or aquired citizenship rights. Eventually there may be some pressure on to settle down within a defined region in the still open spaces of the presumptive territory.

3. There are at least two possible roles for the researcher at the diffusion stage:
a. As external resource person working with individual organizations. I would think that this should be accepted only where a fundamentally new problem is involved or a new type of innovation is attempted.
b. A new role for the researcher at this stage would appear to be at the level of and in relationship to one or more diffusion networks.

There is a need for organizations involved in socio-technical change programmes to develop networks for exchange of experience, information, joint workshops, visits and possibly exchange of or joint use of staff. This is quite different and separate from the type of network which we have been involved in, interrelating research institutions, which has a different type of function. Judging by our own experience, it is important that the networks are initiated by the organizations themselves, and that in this case the role of researchers is in each case defined by joint consultation. This is important at the diffusion stage in order to develop, maintain and protect the autonomy of the organizational change process.

The type of network structures which we find to be emerging stand in marked contrast to the traditional expert directed sensitivity and training conferences, which now appear almost like survivals of an authoritarian culture. The structure of the latter is so clearly in conflict with their ostensive aim, and their message in conflict with their practice. What may be conveyed under these conditions if only unintentionally are manipulative skills.

The advantage to researchers in being linked to networks is that easy and immediate access is obtained to emerging and new trends, innovative approaches to existing problems and to new problems which appear. At the same time research experience is needed to evaluate different types of network and conference structures. In Norway, a network has been formed by a group of firms engaged in socio-technical change projects, which convenes joint workshop conferences when needed and maintains contacts during the intervening period. Over a time, what began as conferences chiefly devoted to lectures, turned into workshops organized by a sponsoring institution which provides the chairmanship, and programme outline. The emerging trend at present is for the member organizations to convene as an autonomous group and to take over more of the responsibility for conference organizations. A similar type of network has emerged between shipping firms engaged in developing new forms of ship organization.

The networks formed are likely to be of a temporary nature, or they may after a while disappear and others are formed instead.

In some cases what occurs is what F. E. Emery calls a flocking. That is, the conditions existing and suitable and visible facilities being available, people with a common task interest come together for one or more days, communicating and working together intensively and then disperse. They may never come together again, or they may flock again and come together at some unpredictable and appropriate time. However generally, during the intervening aggregate state, individual contacts of some type may be maintained.

An interesting example occured when the Institute was approached to organize a day of lectures for elementary school teachers in a borough of Oslo on the topic of democratizing school organizations. As it was known that some of the schools in the region were interested in or had already started with some form of projects, it was suggested that the facilities of a school which would be available for a day should be used instead for workshops. In the event, close to hundred teachers, most of them women, and also a number of senior members from the Ministry of Education spent from morning to late in the evening, exchanging experience and discussing the type of problems encountered and some working on further plans in the development of their projects, discussing possible new ways of working together.

The experience gained so far has shown that the original diffusion model based on the spread of innovation in farming communities has had to be modified. However without the actual experience gained with action research in a number of settings it would scarcely have been possible to test and develop this theory further.

According to this model the innovation should be introduced in farms whose owners are highly respected in the community. If the innovation is visibly successful, at least some other farmers will look over the fence, adopt the innovation and so on. The rate of diffusion will in this case have the shape of an S curve, initially a slow growth, then gathering increasing velocity and finally flattening out again as most if not all farmers in the district have adopted the change.

A recent study in South East Asia (Rochin, 1973) shows that a diffusion curve of this type is obtained in the case of a technical change (one would have to assume that capital investment costs are not too high for the relatively poor farmers, or that some kind of subsidy is available). However, an innovation requiring organizational change did not proceed in this way. The diffusion process in this case did not get beyond an elite group. It is sometimes assumed that the poorer segment of society will tend to be more conservative by nature. However in a case of this type one cannot over-look that costs involved in reorganization, when time can not be spared from just keeping things running. Also the relatively greater uncertainty risks involved in an organizational change which cannot be simply copied, installed and possibly payed off on hire purchase will act as a strong con-servative constraint. A similar type of problem is encountered in medium sized firms which have lost the advantages of a small enterprise and not yet gained the advantage of size. Firms of this type frequently find themselves in a situation where they have to utilize all their efforts just to maintain oper-ations, and without staff positions and time to work through an organi-zational change project. To get out of this constraint, which has been en-countered also in the education project, the initial direction for reorgani-zational change chosen has from the start to satisfy the requirement that some degree of slack is created internally.

Increasingly we have become aware that action research has to create or utilize previously unrecognized 'empty social spaces'. Sometimes as in the case of the above example, the state of the game is that all the pieces appear to be locked and no pieces can be moved. Here a move has to be found to create empty spaces. In other cases, empty unutilized spaces may exist in dimensions which will often be discovered by the participants only as the action research gets on the way. For instance, most societal systems with which we have worked such as manufacturing firms, shipping firms and schools have an aggregate structure, that is there are few or no direct links between the components of the system. In this case the possibility exists for cooperative links to be created which may take the form of more or less regular joint workshops conference or irregular flocking sessions. These have a number of functions.

1. A larger network unit provides the supporting conditions whithin which an autonomous and self-maintaining learning process can be established.
2. The formation of such networks by itself changes and transforms the aggregate structure of the system.
3. Networks especially of disparate component organizations which are loosely structured are less easily encapsulated and tend less to encapsulate themselves.
4. Organizations which are dependent on one another may be able to operate independently of one another as long as none of them changes its mode of functioning. This however will no longer be the case as soon as any one organization on its own alters its mode of functioning in a way

which is inconsistent with the way in which other organizations continue to function.

For instance, if a teacher college starts to provide a different form of education for its teachers, then the new type of teachers may not fit into the conventional schools. And also, if a school starts off to develop a new form of educational organization, then the teachers who come from a traditional teachers college may not be able to cope with this.

It is in fact this condition where in the aggregate state, right down to the teacher in the classroom, the components of the system lock one another, so that none can move ahead on his own, and which is supported by the administrative superstructure, which to a large extent accounts for the difficulties which will be encountered in creating an autonomous organizational change and learning process. Here a way out of the impass has been to create a larger unit of change, to begin with a teacher training college together with a school, which allows the change process to be directively correlated in the way of joint participation in policy formation, partially joint implementation and evaluation of results leading to the next cycle of policy formation which may involve a new group of participants. Similarly at a lower level, the unit of autonomous change has been based on groups of teachers who take over joint responsibility for a larger subject unit, thus making it possible to leave behind practically all the traditional structures of school teaching. (Blichfeldt, 1973, 1975)

What is here referred to as empty spaces are those regions within a social space which lie outside that which is prescribed and that which is forbidden by law and regulations. For instance, cooperative relationships between schools or between teachers are neither forbidden nor required.[1]

Especially in fields such as shipping and schools, laws and regulations exist which were framed relative to the requirements of existing types of work organization. As work organization change, some of the existing laws and regulations will need to be altered. As this generally takes some time and since the new requirements can not as a rule be specified beforehand, the recognition and utilisation of available empty spaces avoids that the process of organizational development comes to a stop, and it may in some cases

1. Discretionary regions are bounded and explicitly recognized and protected regions within the empty space. The prescribed and forbidden regions are bounded. If the extent of these boundaries are overestimated, than they will encompass parts of the discretionary region. The empty unutilized space beyond this does not constitute a boundable region, nor does it form part of what is at anyone time recognized as part of the available social space.

be found that it can be accomodated within if not all, than at least most of the existing constraints. Demonstration experiments are needed to provide both the possibility for evaluating the viability and desirability of new organizational forms, and also to provide the conditions needed for making requisite changes in the legal framework.[1]

The original diffusion model we started off with was based on the assumption that the system has and maintains an aggregate structure, the components are relatively homogeneous, and there exists a status gradient such that if a successful demonstration experiment is introduced at the top of the status gradient then this will, by a process of imitation spread throughout the system as a whole. An additional requirement which may exist is that a critical mass is needed at the demonstration stage in order to trigger off the diffusion process. The Emery, Oeser and Tully model (1958) is more complex and includes a number of additional cognitive and social-psychological variables. In the simplest model of this type, where the rate of diffusion is dependent simply on the number of components (or mass) which has adopted the new pattern, it can be shown mathematically that the rate of diffusion will follow an S surve. However we should not be particularly impressed by this, since unless the process takes on an explosive form then the diffusion curve can not take any other form given that the change process to begin with will for some time involve only a few components and in the end peter out when there are only few components left which retain the original pattern. However it is possible that the rate of diffusion flattens out at an earlier stage or that there may be a sequence of S curves. Whatever turns out to be the case, we will not at the start of the process be able to predict the course which the process will take, and at the end, the type of curve obtained will not by itself enable us to infer very much about the structure of the system and less so about the specific characteristics of the diffusion process.[2] While there are conditions which fairly well corre-

1. In Norway the possibility for dispensations has considerably aided the possibility for developing and testing of new forms of organizations. At the same time given an evolutionary learning process within which change of organizational forms will become more frequent and widespread than this was the case in the past, this raises problems with respect to the functioning and adaptability of the legal and administrative system which it will be necessary to study.
2. However, with some additional information the data obtained could be very useful and in fact essential for a theory of diffusion. In Sweden where by now several hundred firms are said to be engaged in socio-technical projects, it would be possible to find out from where and what type of information was obtained and how this was utilised. In Norway the basic concept employed during the initial diffusion process was that of autonomous or partially autonomous groups which could take over most of the functions

spond to the initial diffusion model, it can not be considered as having general validity. The experiences gained so far may be summarized as follows. Given that the innovation involved requires organizational change then

1. Strategical choices are found to exist at each stage of the process, which shows that the diffusion process does not proceed in an automatic and predictable way after the demonstration stage.

2. The type of strategy chosen at any one time may have consequences which do not become apparent until a later stage. Specifically, the type of strategy which may seem to be optimal at the demonstration stage can be counterproductive during the diffusion stage.

3. Prolonged time should where possible not be spent in the single demonstration experiment stage in order to avoid the consolidation of encapsulation processes which may become difficult to reverse later on. I do not think that we could have done very much better with this in the initial experiments in industry as a prolonged learning period was needed both for the firms involved and for the research team. However as far as the more recent projects are concerned, the indications are that the strategy appropriate for diffusion should be adopted as soon as this becomes possible, by extending single demonstration sites to an appropriate network of two or three units.

4. The aggregate structure of the total system if this exists, need not be taken as a given. Instead the transformation of the aggregate structure can become part of the strategy, by activating networks which may change over time or later on subside and thus alter the characteristics of the diffusion process.

5. In the spread of technical innovations, imitation and adoption of a ready made solution may sometimes be possible. However, in socio-technical changes, where the starting off point is initially only partly known and what

of foremen. In Sweden, where it was possible to go almost directly into the diffusion stage utilizing the Norwegian experience, a more selective approach was used. The basic concepts used were decentralized personnel administration, job redesign, change of supervisory roles, and re-evaluation of rationalization techniques. In practice it was found that firms who began to work with one of these problems could become involved in some of the other problems as well.

is aimed at can not from the start be completely specified, imitation of a ready made solution may not only be inappropriate but may also inhibit the diffusion process. The same type of problem will face the researcher if he adopts or allows himself to become maneuvered into the position of an 'expert' who lets his past experience and theory obstruct his perception of the nature and characteristics of the situation in which he finds himself. In learning, what is difficult and problematical is not so much aquiring knowledge, but to put aside what one thinks one knows. In order to help others to do this, one has to learn to do this oneself.

6. The characteristics of the diffusion process depends on the structure of the total system. In going from manufacturing industry to shipping to education it is not simply the nature of organizations, their tasks and technology that differ, but individual organizations are imbedded in a different total system structure. Thus, in manufacturing industry there is a considerable variety of operations and technology, of markets, of links to the labour market and training requirements, of links to the local community and in the history of the firm. Overall there are generally few if any direct links between firms (as long as they operate as independent units). There is in Norway a strong central trade union.

Within the shipping industry there is far less variety in type of operations and markets. Selective cooperative links exist between individual firms and are also more marked at the national policy making level. In this system where individual firms are generally well informed of what others are doing, demonstration experiments are more highly visible. Unlike manufacturing industry, the shipping industry is governed by detailed laws and regulations affecting both ship design, ship personnel and operations. There are several relatively weak unions with partially conflicting interests.

The school system in Norway is almost entirely State run and under the central authority of the Ministry of Education. There is scarcely any variety of schools, and where this still exists the over-all policy has been to work towards maximum uniformity. Individual schools have scarcely any autonomy. The operation of schools are governed in considerable detail by national laws and regulations and even the local autonomy left is largely lost by rigid planning. This leaves both teachers and pupils with scarcely any apparent possibility for participating in matters affecting the organization and functioning of the school, and the joint participatory councils which have been attempted tend to have more form than content. There are practically no links between schools or to other organizations in the local community. It is fairly easy to point to all the factors which would indicate that getting an 'autonomy project' started and into the diffusion stage, would be very difficult. In fact we were not very hopeful at the start. The positive and supporting conditions have begun to be clearer only as the project got on the way. In this system, demonstration experiments are not highly visible.

7. It took almost 20 years to get from the initial to the diffusion stage in the manufacturing industry project. In the subsequent shipping project this took about 5 years and in the education project which is the most recent one, this outcome is still uncertain. Within Norway, diffusion is at present more rapid in the more recently started projects. It need scarcely be pointed out that these differences can not be accounted for simply by learning within the research team. The various sector systems such as manufacturing industry, shipping and education are clearly not closed systems but are linked in a number of ways both nationally and internationally. At present we have little in the way of systematic comparative studies of the structure and processes within sector systems. We know even less about the characteristics of the large social ecology at the national and at the international level. Here also action research leads us into new areas and can generate data which would not become available in any other way. A discussion at this level can not at present be more than tentative.

Our basic initial hypothesis was that industrial work organization constitute the central region in Western societies so that changes introduced there should spread out and diffuse to other sectors of society either directly or in the form of a model (Emery 1969). This general hypothesis is by now well supported. What is more difficult however is to distinguish and evaluate different strands in the diffusion process, and to take account of diffusion processes at other levels such as changes at the level of political ideology, in the predominant assumptions about human nature, of assumptions which generate authoritarian or bureaucratic hierarchical organizations and assumptions about sex linked roles in society.

While there is no systematic evidence available, marked changes appear to be at present on the way in the work organization of Norwegian families. In the new type of family organization, the husband may do any of the traditional women's tasks (such as feeding the baby at night) and the wife may do any of traditional man's tasks (such as looking after and cleaning the car). What is distinctive is that there is no rigid allocation of tasks. During the weekend, the wife may take on a more traditional role, and a shift in the pattern is expected when the wife stays at home looking after the children. These families have all the characteristics of a composite autonomous group. This type of organization appears to emerge more easily where both husband and wife are both working either before there are children or after they are grown up. In one description of such a family type the term 'samarbeid' (working together) was used which is the term which has been adopted for the Industrial Democracy Project. It would seem that there are here a number of convergent diffusion trends. These changes both in the family and at work are for instance also in line with one of the aims of the women liberation movement. What is significant is not simply the quantitative rate of change, but the fact that these changes are not necessarily looked at as deviant but as a more appropriate if not an ideal type of family organization. Whatever the actual strands in the diffusion process, a change process of this type may come to support the further process of diffusion of new types of work organization in industry and elsewhere.

Both the shipping and the education project are part of the diffusion process from the initial demonstration experiments in industry. In both cases the Institute was asked to come in as a result of requests for initially exploratory studies to see how and to what extent the experience gained in industry could help to initiate a similar type of organizational change. Here we were helped from the start by an agreement that a direct transfer of solutions from industry might not be appropriate nor would this be attempted. In the shipping industry there has apparently been no further influence from outside, and this chiefly since by now Norway is quite a long way ahead in the design and implementation of new forms of ship organization and the correlated design of living quarters.

The situation is rather different in the education project. Here we soon found that the directions which we indicated for changing the content and structure of teaching were in fact in line with general policies which were originally adopted in the 1930's but for which no way of implementation had been found. The changes proposed were not always looked at as being deviant, but were seen by many teachers as being in line with their ideals and consistent also with the aspirations of pupils. (Here, as also in the early coal mining studies, history plays a significant role). We were asked to come in at a time when both members of the Ministry of Education and the Council for Innovation in Education had as a result of experience come to the conclusion that introducing change by means of central directives presented serious problems and they were interested and willing to support the exploration of a more autonomous developmental process at the school floor level.

The experience gained about diffusion processes in a number of settings indicates that a single diffusion model will not be applicable under all situations. Under different system conditions a different set of variables may be relevant and the variables may be related to one another in different ways. For instance, in some cases, imitation may support the diffusion process, in some cases it may block the process, and where the change process involves directively correlated systems it may be irrelevant. Similarly, prior or induced status differences will sometimes support and sometimes hinder the diffusion process and may sometimes, such as in the case of schools of the same type, be largely irrelevant. We have also discussed a case where the diffusion process operates within a given system structure, and one, where in the course of the diffusion process the structure itself may become temporarily or more permanently transformed. Only a small number of different specific theories are likely to be required for purely technical innovations, and a larger number for the type of conditions encountered in the case of organizational and socio-technical change.

It will therefore be necessary to look for a general theory from which each of the possible processes which may occur can be derived (Figure 4.1).

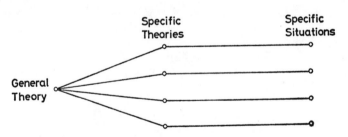

Figure 4.1.

A general theory is not directly applicable to any specific situation and therefore not directly testible. What it does allow is the derivation of different specific theories which have to be empirically tested in different specific situations. The validity of the general theory depends on its capacity to generate all the different theories which can apply and to exclude those which cannot apply under any conditions. An example of a general theory of this type is found in Herbst (1970).

It will be noted that a general theory is not based on isomorphism of different types of system structures, but is needed because the system structures and processes encountered may take different forms.

At present, it may not be difficult to construct a specific theory for the spread of technical innovations in aggregate systems, and this may give some indications for a general theory, from which this specific model should be derivable. The construction of a general theory will have to be left until at least a few empirically tested models become available from which a general theory can be inferred and from which in turn a total set of specific theories would be derivable.

5. Directions of diffusion

Previous chapters reflected backwards on the experience gained in the course of the work democratization project. The aim was to identify different change strategies which have been utilized and the type of obstacles encountered in the early stages of the diffusion process. In the present chapter an attempt will be made to identify directions of development leading into the immediate future.

If in the following a number of actual and potentially negative trends are looked at, then this is not to imply that these appear at the present time to present serious problems. However, it is better to be aware of them, especially where they indicate a need to modify our own approach, rather than to be taken by surprise.

5.1. Mapping diffusion strategies

The model employed is based on linking Thorsrud's concept of 'policy making as a learning process' (1972) with the Emery approach to the 'identification of emerging trends' (1967). When these are linked (*albeit* in a slightly modified and extended form) what is arrived at is a possible method for mapping diffusion strategies.

The Thorsrud concept can be put as follows. What is chosen initially is a general direction of organizational change judged to be acceptable by participants. No end point is at this stage identifiable. What is agreed to, generally by representatives of a set of relevant organizations, is a first step in an indicated direction which is then implemented. The results are jointly evaluated. Possible next steps become then visible and identifiable. A choice of a next step is made, implemented and in turn evaluated at the next stage. Policy making is not defined as specifying a specific goal in the distant future. This is regarded as being unrealistic both in theory and in practice. Instead policy making is defined as saying 'no' to a process of development which is seen by the participants to move in a direction which is not acceptable. Within these limits, policy making is constituted as a continuous learning process.

This describes the essential characteristics of an action research approach. This way of proceeding is specifically appropriate under conditions where the nature of the task is such that the goal is, to begin with, not specifiable in detail, the relevant characteristics of the present are incompletely definable, and the means of implementation are tentative possibilities.[1]

The basic model is shown in Figure 5.1. The direction of change chosen is by implication or explicitly a counter strategy to a recognized trend into the unacceptable region. It is of some relevance for the following that the implementation process may move into a region which may initially appear to be acceptable, but later turns out to be dubious in terms of its future development.

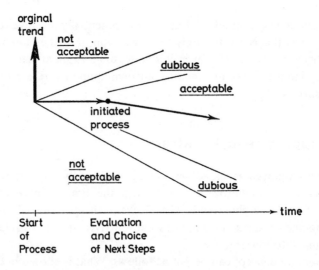

Fig. 5.1. Policy making as a learning process based on Thorsrud (1972).

Among the few statements in the field of social science which on the basis of accumulated experience can be made with some degree of certainty, are that

1. It may be noted that what are relevant characteristics of the present is determined by the aim or direction chosen for the future. If the direction or aim are changed, what are the relevant characteristics of the present will be changed as well. In a somewhat similar way a reinterpretation of the past can change the perceived nature of the present.

1. any strategy has uncertain consequences
2. any steps for moving in a given direction taken initially, will have some countervailing consequences at a later stage,
3. there is always a tendency for parts of a process which is started off to go in a given direction, to go in the opposite direction. Tendencies of this type which may have a positive or negative effect will be referred to as regressive offshoots.

At a later stage it then becomes necessary both to find out where the initiated process has taken us, and also to identify emergent offshoots which have started off in the course of diffusion. We can then make a diffusion strategy map as shown in Figure 5.2.

Here a strategy which initially appeared acceptable, has moved into the dubious region and given rise in the course of diffusion to an identifiable offshoot. The possible future direction of an offshoot in its relation to other on-going or emerging change processes is generally called a scenario. If now the offshoot by itself or together with the scenario indicates relatively clearly that the process is heading towards the non-acceptable region then a correction strategy will be needed which brings at least the process which one has initiated oneself into the acceptable region.

In Figure 5.2 another example is shown where an offshoot goes into the dubious region but one possible scenario points into the non-acceptable region while another points in the direction of the acceptable region. In which direction it may go will depend on which of two alternative types of future contexts will emerge. The best that can be done in this case is to be at least as clear as possible about one's assumptions about the type of future on which the strategy is based, so that the assumptions can where necessary be corrected.

The simplest case might be conceived of as one where a change process is set off under conditions where the rest of the social system is taken to be either constant or changing in terms of a predictable trend. This assumption which underlies most 'rational' planning techniques is a practical impossibility, and would hold only if the social system is an aggregate of isolated elements, so that a change of any one characteristic will not affect others. If this is in practice not the case, then the change process modifies the social context, and in the interaction new properties arise. At the same time the change process may start off offshoots in different directions. As a result more and more external interventions may be implemented. In this way the techniques employed for controlling and stabilizing societal conditions may

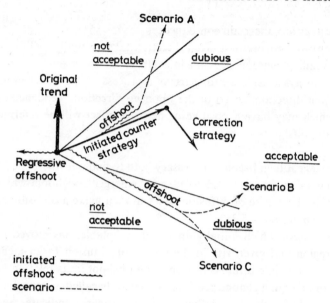

Fig. 5.2. Diffusion strategy map.

lead to a steady increase in turbulent and chaotic conditions. At the same time the techniques of planned intervention, based on the assumptions of predictability and isolated elements, appears to be the only one which is consistent with the mode of operation of centralized bureaucratic hierarchies.

The alternative is the utilization of a stepwise learning process which is consistent with non-bureaucratic and non-hierarchical organizations.

Thus, bureaucratic hierarchical organizations utilizing planned intervention techniques constitute one type of self-sustaining system, and non-bureaucratic, non-hierarchical organizations utilizing policy making as a learning process constitute another type of self-sustaining system. While the former is adapted to a predictable type of environment, the latter is adapted to environments where only tentative predictions for a shorter period ahead are possible.

We have already noted that a change process which is initiated may give rise to a family of offshoots. These may be set off in different social contexts and thus develop different path properties.

In practice the situation becomes more complex, in so far as a given change process occurs within a context where other actual or emerging change process occur. If the initiated process functions as a 'leading part' (Emery, 1967), then a simpler model will be feasible.

The conditions where a formulation of scenarios may be useful is:
1. when a relevant developmental process has entered the dubious region
2. when several actual and emerging developmental processes become interdependent.

The situation then is somewhat like a set of variables all of which are changing and which are interdependent.

Each of the conditions discussed could be modeled by a mathematical formulation which need not be quantitative.[1] However, other approaches can be utilized. Where there are several actual, emergent and potential processes what one can look for is:

1. what kind of consistent structures are beginning to or can emerge
2. what kind of analogical, imaginative and possibly symbolic representations can be identified which underlie the way in which the situation is perceived and structured by participants.

In theory, and for the outsider, a model about the process may be what he is looking for. In practice an understanding of the model which underlies the way in which participants structure the situation will be of more direct relevance.

In any case, any too ambitious systematic model building may be obsolescent even before it is put on paper. The actual situation may change rapidly, and a previously unidentified emergent can qualitatively modify the total process structure. In this case it will be more helpful to use relatively rough maps which can be utilized and modified in the stepwise learning approach.

So far we have looked only at a change process in a forward direction. However, whenever a change process basically affects existing organizational structures, then some regressive offshoots will manifest themselves. Some of these may clearly point into the non-acceptable regions. Others however may provide significant support for a forward movement. This is perhaps just another way of saying, with reference to the Orwellian scenario, that not everything that is new is good and not everything that is old is bad (or the reverse).

Summarizing up to this point, it would seem that present day social

1. Planned interventions may be based on quantitative mathematical models such as prognosis based on linear or exponential trends. A more sophisticated approach is found in the Meadows et al. (1972) model.

science approaches tend to be too restrictive in looking at the present. Action research requires not only identifying and analysing processes extending into the future, but also an understanding of the past history of the social field.[1] This however needs to be carried out in the context of a concrete situation:

5.2. Diffusion map of the work democratization project

Figure 5.3 shows an attempt to map out the diffusion process from the start of the work democratization project in 1962. The main emphasis is on offshoots and their potential future trends. As far as the initiated changes are concerned, only those characteristics which are of particular relevance for the diffusion process are referred to. There are more details which one might wish to put into the diagram, however, as this would clutter up the map, it seems better to take these up in the text.

There are three clusters of offshoots.

These are trends in the direction of:

1. Technocratic types of organization. Basically these are organizations in which engineering type models are used as a universal control technique. This trend is generally easy to identify and not problematical as far as its implications are concerned. The appeal is to effectiveness and rationality of the organization achieved by means of impersonal, machine like, techniques. If a human justification is made, it is terms of 'equality' or in terms of inherent inborn individual differences of ability.
2. Sociocratic types of organization. These are organizations which seek to utilize 'social science techniques' as a universal control method. This trend in its initial stages may be difficult to identify since it can be veiled in 'progressive' and 'enlightended' words. The appeal is to effectiveness of the organization or could be to other societal aims to be achieved by manipulating human needs to given requirements.
3. The third cluster consists of pure offshoots which result when parts of the existing bureaucratic structure are removed. The first of these is regressive de-bureaucratization. For instance job rotation and 'flexibility' may be interpreted to give the supervisor increased power to rotate his subordin-

---

1. An example is the Norwegian EEC referendum. For the opponents, both progressives and conservatives, what became activated as models was the memory of the union with Sweden in the 19th century, and the relationship of the Protestant North with the pope in Rome.

ates around as he sees fit. The indications are that at least in the Scandinavian setting, this trend does not appear to be a serious one. The second offshoot was identified at an early stage by E. Trist (1963) when in the book on autonomous composite groups he used the sub-title 'the loss, rediscovery and transformation of a work culture'.

The technocratic and sociocratic trends appear to be polar opposites. In practice they are more like twins or, to change the analogy like two sides of the same coin, and at times the two approaches can merge almost complelely. For instance 'programmed teaching' is as much consistent with a technocratic model as it is with the principles of Skinnerian conditioning. However, taken by itself each of these trends has distinctive characteristics.

What all three trends within and offshoots towards the non-acceptable region have in common is that they strengthen and reinforce the power of the controller over the controlled, and specifically the first two depend on delegating unquestioned power to professional experts. This clearly indicates the alternative type of strategy which needs to be followed in the direction of work democratization. The possibility of regressive trends in the direction of arbitrary authoritarianism indicates that debureaucratization will not be enough if the existing hierarchical structures are taken as given.

What lies between the technocratic and the sociocratic trend is not a socio-technocratic approach. This, in its prolongation, would lead to an 'enrichment' of the technocratic trend. If utilized, this is at best a dubious first step.

The action research project which got started in Norway in 1962 had as its aim, with the cooperation of the Trade Union Confederation, the Employers' Confederation and the firms concerned, to discover and implement forms of work organization to replace traditional organizational forms based on the controller – controlled principle. The restriction accepted was that a reduction of productivity and efficiency would not be acceptable in the long run.

The only practical model available at the time was the composite autonomous work groups able to function without a foreman or supervisor which had been studied in the British coal mines.

As shown in Figure 5.3 the first steps of the initiated process moved into the dubious region. In the Christiania Spigerverk experiment, the analysis, evaluation, design and implementation were carried out by a professional outside staff. This first attempt to establish an autonomous group in manufacturing industry, which had the characteristics of an experiment, was 'suc-

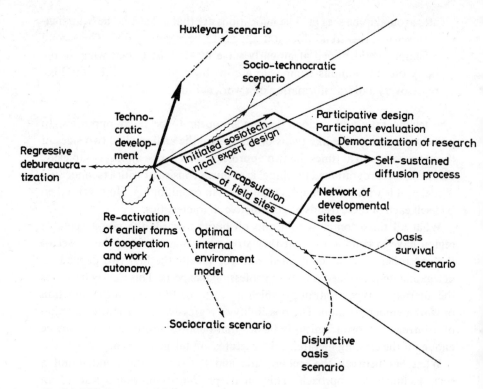

Fig. 5.3. Diffusion map of the work democratization project 1975.

cessful' for the time it lasted. At least within the Norwegian setting there were no subsequent offshoots in the direction of a socio-technical expert model. In the next field sites the first step was the establishment of an internal action group, and it is of some significance for the subsequent process that the staff at Hunsfos took the initiative to establish this group as a vertical slice. At this stage, the external consultant was linked to (at Hydro a member of) the action group, and played an active role in the organization design and evaluation. The field sites were successful and survived, however they did so in an encapsulated form.

Encapsulation was originally encountered as a result of processes within the environment. However there are indications from more recent developments in the US that it may also become actively utilized by an organization as a protective technique. This suggests possible offshoots in the direction of an oasis model.

While the need for corrective strategies became recognized by us in the early 70's, it is only more recently that it becomes apparent that directively correlated developmental changes were occurring within the social field. What had been interpreted as a stagnation phase in Norway after 1968 turns out to have been a latency phase. For some years, quite a few members of the Institute became discouraged about the future prospects of the project. Little was done to push the project in industry further. This in its consequences turns out to have been the best policy. By the time a steady diffusion process got on the way in about 1972 the ownership of the project had effectively passed to and has been maintained by the firms concerned. At least one thing that has happened in the intervening phase is that firms have freed themselves from the dominating influence of the Institute during the initial phase. However, something more has happened, for what seemed strange and exotic ideas in the early 60's has become an approach which in each firm is evolved and rediscovered in its implications in relation to their own specific situation.

At present, apart from firms who work on their own, there is an open forum for members from six factories who each year come together for several four day sessions throughout the year. Each factory sends a slice group composed of line managers, foremen, and shop floor staff including shop stewards.[1] Only a short introduction is given on general principle. Most of the time is spent by each group working on its organizational design problems. The results arrived at are presented in plenum giving both members from other firms and available consultants the opportunity to make comments. In subsequent sessions each team reports on the progress made and works on both the next design stages and further implementation steps.

I had the opportunity of sitting in on the discussions of a work group from a factory which until recently had been a leading exponent of traditional production design and rationalization techniques. I was struck both by the culture change that had occurred and the level of sophistication in working on a bottom-up approach to establish autonomous type groups and find an alternative role for the foreman. In this setting the next level of management was able to discuss how some of their functions could be delegated.

It would appear from the process observed in this group, that one of the reasons why the diffusion process started off rapidly in Sweden in about 1968

1. The vertical slice approach has been adopted as a general principle at present after a visit by Fred Emery. The forum is chaired and organized by Lars Ødegaard who was previously a member of the Trondheim Institute where he worked on the Noboe Project.

was, that at that time, the leading industrial firms were coming to the end of the phase when they had been looking for almost entirely technical solutions. It is only more recently that Norwegian firms began to come to the end of this phase. At the same time, diffusion at present appears to have more the characteristics of a steady growth process.

Since the firm concerned does not have special staff resources or internal consultants for carrying out organizational change projects, the developmental process is dependent on the diffusion of a shared set of principles throughout the organization. This in turn may significantly contribute to the possibility of a long term and self sustained process of developmental change.

Towards the end of the work session, and almost like an echo of a comment made by the miners in Durham almost twenty years earlier, one of the participants suddenly looked around the group and said: 'But is'nt this the way we used to work'. There was a moment of silence, and then the group went on with its task of designing a new work organization.

Part II.

Human foundations of organizational logics

6. Totalitarian logics: the quest for certainty [1]

In the classical approaches to science we seek to understand phenomena and events, which are in some form systematically recorded, in terms of a theory. The objects of our theory are assumed to be passive, and so unable to complain about the way in which we construe or treat them. This approach is not entirely adequate even in the physical and natural sciences. The way in which we apprehend, construe and treat objects depends on the intentions, purposes and aims which we pursue.

The way in which we comprehend and respond to phenomena and events is like Janus, a double-faced process. Looking in one direction it tells us something about what we take to be the nature of the outside world. Looking in the other direction it tells us something about the nature of ourselves.

If we now seek to understand the human and social world, then we need to recognize that unlike objects, every human being has the capacity for construing in his way what he takes to be the nature of the outside world, and in so doing constitutes the structure of himself. It is this actual or potential divergence in the way in which the world may be perceived, interpreted and responded to, which leads to totalitarian logics as a way of seeking to establish uniformity and certainty.

Totalitarian logics can be formulated in terms of a set of assumptions which are taken to be self-evident and beyond doubt. These assumptions, if they are in accord with traditional formal logic, lead to necessary rational logical consequences. The basic assumptions being beyond doubt, then the rational and logical consequences will also be beyond doubt, or so it would seem. What is found, is that the subsequent confrontation of theory with facts leads to irresolvable contradictions, and the ideal quest for certainty on which man may set out in this way with the best of intentions, can turn out to be a treacherous will-o'-the-whisp.

Every rational logic rests on a set of axiomatic assumptions which generate

1. The title *The Quest for Certainty* was used by J. Dewey (1929) for a series of lectures.

a structural system and the mode in which it functions as a consequence. A set of axioms of this type may be described as a *genetic core*. What I wish to indicate by this term is that:

1. While the structural system may be exceedingly complex, it can as a rational structure be generated as a necessary consequence from a small set of axiomatic assumptions.
2. In order to understand the structure and mode of functioning of a system of this type, it is in principle sufficient if the set of axiomatic assumptions from which it is generated is correctly identified.
3. A genetic core, in terms of its consequences, structures the total universe in a comprehensible, meaningful and ideally consistent and unambiguous way.

In the case of totalitarian logics the basic axioms turn out to be what are taken to be self-evident assumptions about human nature. When we examine these further what we find is that we are faced by what may be best described as *mytho-logical systems*.

However, it is not only in totalitarian logics but in any type of logic that the mythical and rational structure are inseparable aspects of the same system. The mythical content is generated by the self-evident assumptions.

Totalitarian logics are consistent with and in fact based on the axioms of formal Aristotalian logic. An essential axiom of formal logic is the 'exclusion of opposites'. Thus, black and white being opposite characteristics, a black object can not be white, and a white object can not be black. In the same way, good and evil being opposite characteristics, a good person can not be evil, and an evil person can not be good. An assumption of this type contributes not only to the construction of a rational logical system, but at the same time generates a myth type world structure.

We create in this way a world in which persons cannot be both good and evil. They must be either the one or the other. As a result the actors in the world drama become in a sense non-human, either super-human or sub-human, either pure angels or utter devils. There is nothing in between. This generates the basis for a Manichaen universe in which the wholly good and the wholly evil stand utterly separate and opposed to one another. There is as yet no necessary condition for conflict. As in Maoist logic a contradictory relationship may or may not be antagonistic. Let us now add the basic assumption that (for all practical purposes) the characteristics of persons are permanent and unchanging. These characteristics may be taken to be inborn, determined genetically or by race. They may be environmentally determined by birth as a member of a specific social class or culture, or they may as in Milton's Paradise Lost have their origin in an act of free choice, which has eternal and irrevocable consequences.

The world constructed at this stage is one where it is not possible for the members of one group to change or be converted to members of the opposing group. There is again as yet no necessary condition for antagonistic conflict. In the Calvinistic doctrine of predestination the elect are certain of their fate and need not trouble themselves about those predestinated for hell. In the Essene sect those who wished to live a pure life segregated themselves from the rest of the world in self-sustaining communities.

It is only by adding as a third injunction the aim of creating a wholly good world that a totalitarian logic results. For if it is assumed that people are inherently either good or evil and that these are permanent characteristics than the creation of a wholly good world becomes achievable only by the complete eradication and liquidation of those who are evil. It is not possible to show within this logic that this end is not attainable. To do so we have to go beyond the totalitarian logic and adopt a dialectic logic.

It may seem almost paradoxical that the totalitarian logic of say Hitler's 'Mein Kampf' may be rational and consistent as far as the logical structure is concerned. The problem does not lie in the logic, but in our assent to or rejection of either the basic assumptions or of the consequences.

An examination of totalitarian logics exemplifies both the subjectivity and essential purposiveness of logical systems. The common characteristic of logical systems is their capacity for arriving at inexorable and necessary conclusions. It is this aspect which makes it possible to employ them to force conviction, leave no room for personal choice (thus their claim to objectivity) and compel specific behaviour, not by direct command, but by apparently free choice which can only lead to one conclusion.

A logical system used for compulsion can gain acceptance in two ways. One way is to identify rationality *per se* with generally accepted values such as truth or effectiveness. In this case the demonstration or conviction of rationality by itself can be used to achieve belief in the inevitable truth of the conclusions and elicit behaviour compliance. Examples are mechanical teaching programs and EDP systems which may be used to control human operators in work organization. Here the participants may not be given the chance to examine critically or to modify the premises on which the logic is based.

Compulsion is based both on the acceptance of the rationality of the procedure as a sufficient guarantee for truth, and the choice of specific criteria for effectiveness which the procedure is claimed to achieve. This is probably one of the most effective means for behaviour control which can be devised since it gains acceptance for premises from which necessary consequences follow, without presenting the premises from which the conclusions follow. At the same time the rationality of the steps by which the conclusions are achieved are guaranteed by the machine and thus not subject to critique apart from the irrelevant possibility of a machine error. Here the purpose is to create a structure which compels specific behaviour, and leaves no room for counter-strategy. The purposive character of logic is in this case particularly clear. In the Socratic method on the other hand the premises can be judged against the conclusions. The purpose is to free the mind from programmed unexamined thinking.

In the political field, totalitarian logics are applied in a different way. Here the premises are treated as self-evident, and given the necessary truth of the premises, then the conclusions together with their action imperatives necessarily follow. Given the evident premises, then anyone who can think logically or follow a logical argument will arrive at the conclusions which it is sought to implement. Here some degree of intelligence and education far from being a hindrance is a necessary prerequisite, since applying the logic oneself and thus arriving self at the conclusions will carry more personal conviction than conclusions which are imposed by decree.

The totalitarian logics which we shall examine are similar to Aristotelian logic in that the premises are taken to be self-evident and similar also in the type of assumptions which are accepted as self-evident. If we dismiss the claim that any kind of logic is self-validating, then there are two criteria for acceptance or rejection.

1. We can examine the premises for their empirical validity.
We may in this case find that Aristotelian premises instead of having universal validity may have restricted empirical validity. In this case a particular logic can like any theory be rejected. However, it is not possible to regard logic simply as an empirical science. This is the case since some of the basic premises in so far as they provide the ground for our thinking and judgement, can not always be simply judged as being right or wrong. In this case, given that no empirical criteria for judging a specific set of premises exists then.

2. *the premises which generate a specific logic are judged in terms of whether the action consequences are consistent with our aims and values.*
The goodness of our aims and values cannot be judged in terms of any logic, but only in terms of our understanding of the personal consequences for ourselves and other of our judgements and actions.

We shall in the following start with building more systematically one of the simplest types of genetic core for a totalitarian logic, which can then be expanded or modified to the point where it can be applied to the coding of data and testing of hypotheses. A totalitarian logic does not necessarily imply that the basic axioms have a totalitarian character. *It is only a specific conjunction of axioms which generates in terms of its action implications a totalitarian structure.*

We shall for a start consider the simplest type of Manichaen logic, which is consistent with the axioms of Aristotelian logic. The world model generated by this logic is one which generates two classes of persons. Those who are good and only have good characteristics, and those who are evil and only have evil characteristics. There is nothing in between. It further excludes (for all practical purposes) the possibility that an evil person may become good or vice versa.[1] The axiom set is to begin with quite rudimentary. However, it provides the basis for a totalitarian logic. The chief characteristic of Manichaen logic is that it generates a large number of contradictory patterns which are excluded as impossible. Thus it cannot account for the possibility that a good person may do an evil act. Totalitarian logics are arrived at if, instead of treating contradictions as impossible, a method is provided to resolve all (apparent) contradictions. This becomes possible by making a distinction between appearance and reality.

Suppose, an evil person is found to do something good. Consistency can then be established as follows. Since an evil person can only do evil, his good act is only *apparently* good, but in *reality* evil. The distinction made between appearance and reality can thus be used to save the logic.

The Aristotelian axioms contain another possibility for the resolution of contradictions which does not lead to a totalitarian logic. A distinction can be made between inherent (real) characteristics and accidental characteristics.

1. In Milton's 'Paradise Lost' this possibility, although a most unlikely event, is presentde in the fall of the angels. However, consistent with this logic the transition is instantaneous since there are no in-between stages. If free transition in either direction is permitted, then this constitutes a change in one of the axioms of the genetic core and a move in the direction of a logic, where no characteristic is taken to be permanent.

If a good person does an evil act, then this can be regarded as an accident. The axiom that a good person only does good (intentionally) is then retained. A totalitarian logic excludes accidental characteristics. Its aim is to exclude all events which are either ambiguous or do not form part of a causal determinate structure. If say a machine in a factory has broken down, leading to a stop in production, the act is classified as evil and the immediate implication is that it must have been caused by a person with evil intentions (who carried out sabotage). A causal determinate structure for all possible events is maintained and consistency is established as a necessary law of nature within this type of world model.

Manichaen type logic

Basic axioms

1. *Quality axiom:* Persons are good or evil. They cannot be both.
2. *Consistent Attribution Axiom:* A good person can only have good characteristics, and an evil person can only have evil characteristics.

Subsidiary axioms

3. *Permanence axiom:* Personal qualities are permanent and not subject to change. That is, persons are inherently either good or evil.
4. *Identification axiom:* Personal qualities and characteristics are identifiable without error. That is, it is possible to determine without error both whether a person and his characteristics are good or evil.

The basic axioms generate the logical structure. The subsidiary axioms determine how the structure operates. The above type of Manichaen logic appears to be the most restrictive which can be formulated. It leaves only two person-characteristics patterns as empirically realisable, while all the rest are impossible, as shown in Table 6.1.

Manichaen type logic eliminates by its axioms all possibility of inconsistencies and within it no uncertainties, ambiguities and conditions of cognitive imbalance can arise, and it is this which is the purpose of this logic.

   In the totalitarian type logic which will be considered next the first three axioms are retained, but the validity of the fourth axiom is rejected. That is, it is asserted that we can not always be certain that a person is good or evil or that an act is good or evil. We can misinterpret an event or we can be deceived.

Table 6.1. Person-characteristics implications of the Manichaen type logic.

Person		Characteristics	
good	implies	good	Possible
evil	implies	evil	
good		evil	
evil		good	
good and evil		—	Impossible
—		good and evil	

What is introduced here is a distinction between appearance and reality.

At first sight it would appear that this modification will considerably weaken the power of the logic. However, quite the reverse is true. In conjunction with the first three axioms what is now achieved is a total logical account of all patterns of events including those which previously had to be rejected as impossible. For instance, assume that an evil person is observed to carry out an act which is judged to be good. This is inconsistent with the second axiom. However, in the totalitarian logic this can now be accounted for. Either the person is really evil in which case the act is pseudo-positive and thus in reality evil, so we have been deceived. Or the person is really good and although the act may appear to be evil, since a good person can only do good, the act is really good. In this way every inconsistent pattern of events can be transformed into a consistent pattern which satisfies the basic set of logical axioms. What is achieved is an explanation for every possible event, the resolution of all ambiguities, and the achievement under all conditions of a state of cognitive balance. And this is at least one of the purposes of a totalitarian type logic.

Totalitarian type logic

Basic axioms

1. *Quality Axiom:* Persons are good or evil. They cannot be both.
2. *Consistent Attribution Axiom:* A good person can only have good characteristics and an evil person can only have evil characteristics.

Subsidiary axioms

3. *Permanence Axiom:* Personal qualities are permanent and not subject to change.

4. *Inconsistence Resolution Axiom:* If a pattern consists of inconsistent
attributions (Axiom 2) that is, both positive and negative characteristics,
then either the positive characteristics are pseudo-positive or the negative
characteristics are pseudo-negative.

Table 6.2 shows how Axiom 4 leads to a resolution of inconsistencies and
establishes cognitive balance.

Table 6.2. Person-characteristics implications of the totalitarian type logic.

Person		Characteristics	Consistency transformation	
good	implies	good		
evil	implies	evil	consistent	
good		evil	implies either good and pseudo-evil or pseudo-good and evil	Possible
evil		good	implies either evil and pseudo-good or pseudo-evil and good	
—		good and evil	implies either good and pseudo-evil or evil and pseudo-good	
good and evil		—	—	impossible

A logic if we accept it, is not something which stands objectively outside
of us. It is not something which stands separate and apart from us. In so
far as we accept a given logic we become part of it. It is only in so far as we
become part of it that a logic functions as a determinate purposive system
which automatically decides for us our attitudes and actions.

A totalitarian logic if it is accepted, leaves the choice only between
identifying ourselves as good or evil persons. However, this logic which is
fully deterministic, does not leave this open for free choice, since these
qualities are taken to be inherent and permanent.

The present logic if it is accepted, decides whether we are in fact good and
evil. In Calvinistic Theology the inherent qualities are predetermined, we
can only discover them and not decide them ourselves. In National Socialist
ideology, inherent qualities were determined by the parents' race, and in
Stalinist Russia they could be determined by the parents' social class.

It will be noted from Table 6.2 that the logic is symmetrical so that it works
in the same way whether the identification is with a good or evil person.[1]

1. Heider (1946) shows that in the study of cognitive balance a reversal of the logical
form is obtained depending on whether the person likes or dislikes himself. For other
discussions of cognitive consistency see Newcomb (1953) and Festinger (1957).

In the following discussion of inconsistence transformations, we assume that the reader identifies with a good person.[1]

Assume that:
An evil person does a good act.

To establish consistency, there are two possibilities. Either, the person is in fact evil, and the act is pseudo-positive, that is he has deceived us into thinking that the act is good when in fact it is evil, which is in any case just what an evil person would do.

Or, the person is pseudo-evil and in fact good. He may for instance as part of his mission join the enemy and deceive them. He is therefore only apparently an evil person, but really a good person, who is working for us.

A good person does an evil act.

Either the person is pseudo-positive, that is he has deceived us into thinking he was good, but now by doing an evil act he unmasks himself and shows himself to be evil. Therefore, since he is intrinsically evil also his previous acts, which we thought were good, were in fact evil.

Or the person is in fact good. Since a good person cannot do what is evil, the act is only apparently evil and in reality good.

The totalitarian set of axioms thus makes it possible to derive a logical and rational explanation for every event. It does so by introducing a distinction between appearance and reality and changing appearances in order to make them consistent with the conclusions which follow from the set of self-evident axioms. This strategy, however, creates its own difficulties. The totalitarian logic which was designed to give an unambiguous answer to what is right or wrong, produces in the above case answers which cannot both be right and wrong, and the logic does not tell us which of the two alternative ways of resolving inconsistencies is correct.

In order to find a way out of the impasse, totalitarian logic has to find a decision rule which makes it possible to determine which of the two alternative ways of resolving an inconsistent state is correct. The trouble is that no such decision rule which provides absolute certainty can be formulated

3. The observer is always part of the logic which he employs, since it is he who makes the conceptual distinction. Spencer-Brown (1969) shows that the conceptual distinction and the person who makes the conceptual distinction are not only interchangeable, but in their form identical.

in a way which is consistent with the basic axioms. Totalitarian logic which seeks to achieve complete certainty thus fails to achieve this on the basis of its own premises.[1]

One possibility is to introduce a decision rule based on the cost of making an error. The assumption is made that it is far more dangerous to mis-identify a person who is evil, because an evil person is dangerous and can do damage. However, to misidentify a good person will do little harm. There-fore it is much better when in doubt to assume that the person is evil.

This can be put in the form of the following principle.

Decision rule

In case of an inconsistent pattern if in doubt which of the alternative ways for resolving the inconsistency is correct, choose the assumption that the person is in fact evil.[2]

This creates the logic of the mediaeval witch trials, the wartime German SS formations and of the state security service during the Russian Stalinist period.

However, it is also possible to formulate another decision rule based on finding a criterion which will make it possible to decide without doubt who is a good and who is an evil person. This was the problem encountered by the National Socialist regime when it was found that it was not always possible to decide whether a person was a Jew or not and led to Göring's well known edict, which rather literally translated goes 'who is a Jew and who is not, it is I who decide'.[3]

1. The basic motivation for any kind of authoritarian logic is just this need to achieve complete certainty, so that any kind of ambiguity and uncertainty becomes painful, if not intolerable.
2. The decision rule in its reverse form goes back to Pascal's famous and almost irrefutur-able argument for accepting the truth of Christianity which can be put as follows. When the gain is infinitely large and the odds against finite . . . we must bet everything. In the present case, the decision rule is, if the risk is slight and the possible loss very high, do not take the risk.
3. The Red Queen in Lewis Carrol's 'Alice in Wonderland' gives another good example of this attempt to solve a dilemma. The irrationality of the story is the result of a conse-quent application of classical logical principles. The author apparently believed that this would be more easily understood by children than by adults. It is quite important here to distinguish between non-rationality, that is lack of ability or rejection of logical consistent thinking, and irrationality which results if what is empirically observable is rejected in favour of what is theoretically true. It is here that we can find one of the sources for the non-biological more or less pathological mental disorders. The possibility of regaining mastery over the logic which one has constructed exists in so far as insight is gained into the motivational conditions which lead to the acceptance of the basic axioms which generate a particular logic.

The problem now is that both decision rules are feasible, but if they are both used, they lead to inconsistent ways of resolving inconsistencies. At this point the totalitarian logics can get caught in irresoluble internal contradictions.

We note that either strategy of conflict resolution leads to a primitivation of the logic.

The totalitarian logic, where it cannot cope with its internal contradictions, is forced to fall back on to the more primitive Manichaen logic which constitutes its basic core.[7] The Manichaen logic as we saw previously, simply negates the empirical validity of what is inconsistent with its principles. The validity of the empirical given is where necessary negated if it conflicts with the theory. The totalitarian logic does not negate the validity of empirical reality as such, but assumes to begin with that if there is a disagreement between theories and events, then the reason for this lies in that we have misinterpreted what we have observed, and then utilizes the theory to reinterpret the facts. It is in this way that the theory is maintained incontrovertible.

What has not yet been shown is how the totalitarian logic is related to totalitarian types of social organization. There is up to this stage nothing in the logic itself which generates an antagonistic conflict. We are reminded here that there are two ways of representing the after-death world. In one, the inhabitants of heaven and hell each live in their own world, that is, we have an apartheid system, in the other, the forces of good stand in antagonistic conflict with the ultimate aim of the complete annihilation of the evil.

Let us now add to the basic axioms of totalitarian logic the following injunction.

Injunction: Let there be a world free of evil.
By itself the injunction may appear idealistic, perhaps even harmless, it is after all what we may all wish for. In conjunction with the totalitarian axioms it becomes murderous. Since evil is an intrinsic characteristic of a class of persons, a wholly good world can result, only by the complete and utter liquidation of the evil.

---

1. We may note here the possibility of deriving the principle stated by Lewin that frustration leads to regression. This like other psychological principles is not universally valid, but depends on the type of logic on which the individual's behaviour is based. At the same time once the logic is known, psychological principles of this type can become derivable, and it is possible in the present case to state both the type and direction of primitivation.

Practically all the modern totalitarian ideologies and regimes started with this idealistic injunction linked with a set of totalitarian axioms[1].

The aim of creating an all-good world is consistent with the axioms of a totalitarian logic. It is the difficulty of achieving this state which leads to a higher-order dialectic logic. In the dialectic logic the good by the act of defining itself simultaneously creates its opposite as that which it excludes.[2]

This insight is already implicit in the earliest forms of Indo-German mythologies. In the battles between the opposing hosts, neither side gains a complete victory.

What we thus find is a hierarchy of logics, the Manichaen, the totalitarian and finally the dialectic. In each case the higher-order logic is developed to overcome the contradictions of the earlier logic.

This hierarchy of logics which has the Aristotelian axioms as its basis, constitutes a central core in Western thought. It is possible to show that there exists a hierarchy of logics also in Eastern, specifically Buddhist thought, which is however of a fundamentally different nature and can be looked at as an inverse hierarchy of logics.

Both have as their points of departure Aristotelian type axioms taken as self-evident propositions. However, while Western thought follows the direction of adding additional principles in order to save the theory from contradictions by empirical givens, the Buddhist thought goes in the opposite direction by negating, one after the other, the axioms on which logic is based. In Western thought, if a contradiction is encountered, the theory is patched up by adding new axioms or modifying others. In Buddhist thought the contradictions generated by any set of logical axioms are used to destroy specific axioms and ultimately the logic itself and thus to transcend it. The basic difference is that in Western thought ultimate truth is generally taken to be intellectual, that is something that can be put in the form of symbols on a piece of a paper. The theory is the primary aim and the empirical givens of secondary importance and valuable only in so far as they contribute to theory formulation.

1. There is one other way in which totalitarian regimes can be established this time without mass support. Both the Chinese legalists, who helped to establish the first short-lived state covering the whole of China in the 3rd century B.C. and Hobbes in his Leviathan, written in support of monarchic rule in the 17th century, developed a very similar form of what might be called authoritarian logic based on the axiom that all men are intrinsically evil.
3. Spencer-Brown (1970) takes the operation of cleavage of the void, which produces the form and what is outside the form, as the basic form for the formulation of the principles of logic. It is shown in chapter 7 that, alternatively, starting with a triadic set of undefined elements which are definable in terms of one another, it is possible to derive the principles of logic and also the basic concepts of system dynamics.

In Buddhist thought, truth does not lie in any kind of theory. A theory can be used as an instrument to achieve understanding of the empirical givens and once this has been achieved, the theory becomes dispensible. Truth does not lie in the theory. This would be to confuse the tool which one uses for what one seeks to achieve. A theory as a set of symbols on a piece of paper is after all no more than a set of phenomena not different from any other kind of phenomena. In that case, how can any particular set of phenomena be taken to represent an absolute truth?

Implications for psychological theory

The investigation up to this stage suggests a possible way of accounting for observed variations in behaviour principles. Each of the types of logic considered so far structures the world in a particular way. The different types of structure are each determinate and have necessary causal and behavioural implications. They define both the person who makes use of the logic and his environment in a particular way. Each logic thus generates and makes it possible to deduce specific types of behaviour principles, and to show how behaviour principles which apply within one type of logic do not necessarily apply in another one.[1]

Thus we found that there is one kind of logic where the principle of cognitive balance applied to inconsistent events does not operate. In the Manichaen logic, inconsistent events are excluded as impossible. In fact the function of this logic is to avoid any kind of uncertainty which could result from inconsistency between facts and theory. In other words, behaviour based on the Manichaen logic utilizes suppression as a mechanism of defence.

In the totalitarian logic the principle of achieving cognitive balance by altering perceived events to achieve consistency reigns so to say supreme. Wherever an apparent inconsistency is observed, the facts are transformed and reinterpreted in order to save the theory. The aim is to achieve a uniform immutable determinate logic which removes all uncertainty and within which all events become comprehensible. Behaviour in this case utilizes distortion as a mechanism of defense, and behaviour is based on the distorted

1. It is of course possible to reject logic and science. However, if we do so, we overlook that we are as much bound by what we reject as by what we accept. In fact we are more deeply bound by what we reject than by what we accept. For, that which we accept can be transcended by insight and understanding, but that which we reject and repress is beyond conscious control. Psychoanalytically, the lifting of repression by itself is not a cure, it only opens up a possibility for cure.

representation of the empirical given. Since the empirical given is already to begin with apprehended within the categories of the logic itself, the contradictions arise as a consequence of the logic.

Phenomena as such are neither inconsistent nor contradictory. It is our way of apprehending phenomena conceptually within a structure we establish to achieve specific aims, that leads to inconsistencies and contradictions and to ways of finding our way out of contradictions.

Logic and science can be used for the purpose of achieving greater certainty, prediction and control of our environment. In this case this purpose determines the type of logic and science we develop. The structure we develop in turn generates new conditions for actualizing our aims and elaborating the process of conceptual structure building.

Logic and purpose are mutually dependent on one another. Logic presupposes a purpose or intent, and purpose and intent can manifest itself only by means of and in terms of a logical structure within which causality principles operate. One can not exist nor be understood without the other.

To act rationally in terms of a given logic without understanding the premises on which it is based is to act blindly and to be unfree. To understand the premises means that one is able to accept or reject the logic, to use it or to leave it. This is not simply an intellectual task. The purpose or intent of logic and science are not found within the structure of logic itself however far we look, nor obtained by rational elaboration.

What distinguishes man from animal is his capacity for self-reflection. In the words of Chardin (1959) man can know that he knows. He is capable of formulating and understanding the causal and logical structures which unfold in his relationship with his environment. This is the first stage in a process of liberation. It is like having freed one leg but still being stuck with the other. In psycho-analytic terms, the ego feels that it is in full control, without realizing that it functions as a blind servant of the id. At this stage the outer world appears more or less translucent, real and comprehensible, and the inner world appears opaque, impenetrable and more or less unreal.

The specifically human does not lie only in what has been achieved, but in its potential for going beyond. The first stage is necessarily extravert, outgoing, concerned with the conceptual and empirical understanding of the outer world. The next stage goes in the reverse direction, a swimming against the stream to discover the one who is engaged in theory creation.

Used in this sense, the aim of science becomes therapeutic and liberating. It becomes in the course of reflecting on the theories which we create, an understanding of ourselves, and through the understanding of ourselves, the world in which we live.

At this stage the concern is not with the creation of theories, but just the reverse, that is, an understanding and becoming conscious of the purpose of the assumptions and theories with which we build our world.

7. Foundations for behaviour logic

7.1. Introduction

Feelings, desires, intentions and purposes appear to us to constitute part of our subjective experience, unrelated if not opposed to the structure of logic and the forms in which the world appears to us to be given objectively.

And yet, the structures of logic and rational science can not come into existence independently of our personal intents and purposes, which generate the forms in which we come to experience and apprehend the world. For does the infant know that in making its first intentional distinction between itself and its surroundings, that in this simple act he has generated in its consequences the whole field of logic?

The task of behavioural logic is to trace the relation between our intentions and the conceptual and rational forms in terms of which we perceive and respond to ourselves and the environment back to the point where these have their common origin. I use the term intention rather than purpose, since the resultant consequences of our intentions, may not be known by us at the time we act. And also later on, at the time we encounter the consequences of our actions, we may not know who was responsible for them.

7.2. The origin of concepts

The point of departure is a world which is void of all comprehensible characteristics. Assuming that we now wish to construct a world which may be apprehended in terms of distinctions, such as subject and object, object and environment, finiteness and infiniteness, existence and non-existence, which is capable of functioning as a dynamic system, and at the same time structured by a consistent logic, then the question is, what is the minimal requirement which is sufficient for a world of this type to be generated.

There are basically three major theoretical approaches which have been utilized in Western thought to understand the nature of concepts and structures in terms of which the world is apprehended.

Platonic theory takes as its point of departure that both concepts and also logical and mathematical principles can not be more than approximately realised in the world of phenomena. Since, however, both concepts and logic and mathematical principles themselves do not suffer this disability, it is assumed that these exist independently in a rational ideal world. An alternative possibility is to consider concepts not as given *a priori*, but as part of an independently generated system of constructs.

Positivistic theories take as their point of departure that logical and mathematical principles are empirically discoverable. Therefore these principles exist independently of ourselves in the objective world. Here there are two possibilities. Either these laws exist in a perfect state in the objective world, in which case any observed deviation can be accounted for as being due to experimental or measuring error, or these laws are stochastic and generated by chance factors as an objective fact.

Kantian theory takes as its point of departure that the basic categories of logic, time and space are neither given nor found in the external world. These categories therefore are taken to be inherent constituents of the mind which then apprehends the phenomal world in terms of these categories.

Each of these theories vary as to where the basic concepts in terms of which the world is organized and structured are located. They may be located in an ideal *a priori* world, or a system of constructs, in the external world or in the internal world, existing objectively or subjectively. However, there is one thing which all the above theories have in common. Each theory starts off with a dichotomy which splits the world into two distinct systems. In Platonic type theories, a distinction is made between the world of phenomena and a world of concepts or constructs. In both materialist and idealist type theories, a distinction is made between an external or objective world and an internal or subjective world.

It is in this context that a discovery by Spencer-Brown (1969) turns out to be a remarkable step forward in the history of Western thought. He finds that the making of a primary distinction, which is the unexamined given in each of these theories, is by itself sufficient to generate the structure of logic. If then the primary distinction, say into an internal and external world is made, and this by itself is sufficient to generate the structure of logic, then the structure in terms of which phenomena are apprehended can be located neither in an internal or subjective world nor in an external or objective world, and in this case both idealist and materialist type theories can be rejected.

The work of Spencer-Brown has clearly ramifications in almost all branches of human thought, and is likely in time to lead to basic reformulations of Western philosophies. In the present chapter an attempt will be made to take this concept of a primary distinction to a more fundamental and general level. The route taken through this problem is both to explore the common genetic basis of logic and behaviour theory, and at the same time arrive at a definition of some basic general system concepts.

7.3. The primary distinction

The form of the primary distinction is shown in Figure 7.1.

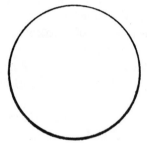

Figure 7.1.

The primary distinction is expressible as a cleavage of an empty space and defined as a crossing of the first distinction. It is in crossing the first distinction that what is the form (the inside) and what is not the form (the outside) is generated together with the boundary which distinguishes the inside and the outside. The Spencer-Brown calculus makes then use of only this single operation 'cross' denoted by ⌐ . This operation leads to the formulation of two axioms. According to *axiom 1*, if the instruction to cross the boundary is repeated, then the end result is no different from a single crossing.

However, if the boundary is crossed and then crossed again (in the reverse direction), then according to *axiom 2* the original state, where no form or boundary exists, is reproduced so that

$$\neg\!\!\lceil \; = $$

where   denotes the empty space in which no distinctions exist. It can
then be shown that these two axioms are sufficient to generate the structure
which corresponds to symbolic and sentential logic.

Unlike formal logic which starts off with a set of elements and operations
as given and links these together to generate different structures, Spencer-
Brown provides a more fundamental psycho-logical approach which allows
an operational interpretation at successive levels.

Psychologically, it implies that the primary distinction made by the
infant between himself and his environment may be sufficient to generate the
conceptual and logical structure in terms of which he later comes to apprehend the world in which he finds himself. These structures therefore may not
need to be assumed to pre-exist either in the external world nor internally,
since the distinction between the internal and the external is already by itself
sufficient to generate the structure of logic. What the infant learns is then
not as Piaget (1953) assumes a correspondence between an independent
system of logic and the emergent structure of his operations. Instead what
the infant discovers and learns in his operational encounter with his sur-
rounding world will be the consequence of the primary distinction which he
has made between himself and his environment.

This then implies that any organism which has come to the stage of making
a distinction between itself and its environment will be capable of operating
in some form of at least rudimentary logic. Organisms capable of generating
a conditioned response to a stimulus appear to lie on this borderline. Human
beings are capable of generating far more complex types of logical structure
and are able to build these into conceptual logical systems and into isomor-
phic mechanisms, which may then be believed to have some form of independent existence.[1]

A comprehension of the dependence of logical and conceptual structures
on the primary distinction between the self and the environment points at
the same time to the possibility of transcending logical and conceptual
structuring as the only realisable mode of knowledge.

While derivation of logical and conceptual structure from the primary
distinction is demonstrable, the generation of the primary distinction starting

---

1. Taken one step further, this can easily lead to the belief that there is no conceivable
difference between a mechanical mechanism and a human being.

off with a world in which as yet no conceptual elements are given to begin with remains problematical.[1]

In the following it will first of all be shown that the validity of the concept of a primary distinction can be more easily demonstrated if we reverse the procedure. To do so we will adapt a different mode of representation than the one introduced by Spencer-Brown. Instead of representing the primary distinction as a single unified operation, we will instead utilize a representation of it as a triadic set of elements

$$[p, q, r]$$

7.4. Reversing the primary distinction

Spencer-Brown describes the state which is free of any distinctions as an empty space. It may be thought that this state is essentially nothingness or perhaps an infinite space. This, however, is demonstrably not the case. Figure 7.2 shows three possible triadic sets which in their form are obtainable from a primary distinction at the stage where a specific characteristic can be attributed to the inside and outside of the distinguished form.

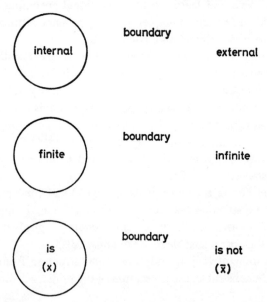

Figure 7.2.

2. Spencer-Brown mentions that his procedure initially was in fact to work backwards from the principles of logic to the simplest conceivable operational basis which could be identified.

The first triadic set is given as

[*inside, outside, boundary*].

It is easily seen that if the boundary is removed, then this is sufficient for the original state prior to the existence of a distinction to be obtained. With the removal of the boundary, a distinction between inside and outside is no longer possible. The same result is obtained if either the inside or the outside is eliminated, for then also the other two components of the triad disappear as well.

Another way of re-establishing the original state is by letting inside and outside become identical and undistinguishable. In this case the boundary disappears.

The primary distinction thus generates a triad of co-genetic components. That is, the three components come into existence simultaneously. Further, the original state prior to the distinction is re-established if either

1. One component of the triad is eliminated, or
2. Two components of the triad (excluding the boundary) become identical.

The second triad in Figure 7.2 has the form:

[*finite region, infinite region, boundary*].

Here again if the boundary is taken away we return to the original state. The original state can thus not be characterized as being infinite, since the characteristic of being infinite does not come into being without the simultaneous coming into being of that which is finite. The original state can therefore not be defined as being either finite or infinite.

Having on occasions explained to some friends and colleagues the nature of the primary distinction, I found that they have no difficulty in seeing that if the boundary is taken away, then both inside and outside disappear. When then asked what is left if the boundary is removed they invariably respond: 'Well then, what is left is nothing". In that case it will appear as if the triadic set consisting of inside, boundary, and outside has been created out of nothing. This also, however, is not the case.

Consider the triad in the form:

[*being, non-being, boundary*].

In traditional logic, these would be denoted by $x = $ is and $\bar{x} = $ is not. If again the boundary is taken away, it is clear that what remains is neither something nor nothing, since the distinction between 'is' and 'is not' can not be made until a primary distinction has been made.

The original state prior to a distinction having been made is thus neither finite nor infinite, neither something that exists nor something that does not exist. It is entirely free of any distinguishing characteristics. However, once a primary distinction has been made, a conceptually apprehendable world comes into existence, within which it becomes possible to say that something exists or does not exist. That it is finite or infinite, that it, belongs to oneself or somebody else.

Starting off from the state in which no distinctions exist, the primary distinction creates a co-genetic triad of components. This triad is the irreducible atomic element of any conceptual system. No one or even two of the component can exist independently. It is therefore in no way possible to define a single concept. Nor is it possible to define a pair of concepts in the form of a duality. The triad is the only and minimal form within which definition of its components is possible. Thus the triad generated by the primary distinction represents the minimum definitional unit.

In the following we shall attempt to develop a behavioural logic using as the starting point a triad of undefined components which are definable in terms of one another.

It will be shown that this is sufficient to derive as consequences the two principles formulated by Spencer-Brown, together with the basic forms of logic and mathematics. It becomes at the same time possible to derive the basis conceptual structures in terms of which the characteristics of the environment are apprehended and to show that each of these constitute dynamic processes.

7.5. The basic axiom of behaviour logic

The point of departure is a world in which nothing definable exists, and which is thus void of any distinguishable characteristics. The characteristics of the primary distinction which as we have seen leads to the simultaneous genesis of three distinguishable components can be stated in the following axiom:

The primary conceptual unit is given as a triad of distinguishable undefined components, which are definiable in terms of one another.

In the following we shall investigate whether this axiom is sufficient to generate the basic concepts in terms of which the phenomenal world is apprehended together with the basic structure of logic and mathematics.

In order to make derivations from the basic axiom possible we shall to begin with need to define the concept of a pair and of an individual component. This can be done as follows.

The triad of undefined components denoted by m, n, p, can be represented in the form

[m, n, p]

This triad is equivalent to a primary distinction. We now make a further distinction within the triad. As shown in the example in Figure 7.3, in whatever way we do this we will always arrive at a pair of components and an individual component. For if a pair of components is enclosed then what is excluded is an individual component, and if an individual component is enclosed then what is excluded is a pair of components. If however the triad as a whole is enclosed, or if none of the components have been enclosed, then no distinction has been made which is contrary to the instructions given

Fig. 7.3. Results obtained by making a distinction within a triad.

The distinction made leads to three possible pairs and three possible single components shown below:

m n	m
m p	n
n p	p

The distinction made will at the next stage make it possible to obtain a representation of a definitional unit.

If we wish to demonstrate the validity of the distinction made, then we have to show that it has generated a triad of components consistent with the basic axiom. The easiest way to do this is to go back to Figure 7.3, and in each case to take the boundary away. In this case, both the pair and the individual components which have been created disappear simultaneously. That this is a necessary property of a triadic unit is shown by the theorem discussed in the next section.

7.6. Conditions for the existence of distinguishable Components

That which has no distinguishable characteristics is denoted by the sign φ.

If in a triad of components, any two or more components are not distinguishable then this is denoted by the equal sign $=$.

Thus:

$$m = n$$

means that m and n are not distinguishable.

Given the triad:

$$[m, n, p]$$

Assume that p is not a distinguishable component and thus $p = \varphi$.

Then the triad takes the form:

$$[m, n, \varphi]$$

Now, assume that in the triad $[m, n, p]$. The components n and p are not distinguishable, so that $n = p$. Then also in this case there remain only two distinct components and the triad takes the same form:

$$[m, n, \varphi]$$

However according to the basic axiom, the condition for any one component to be distinguishable and thus have definable characteristics is that it forms part of a triad of distinguishable components. Therefore in both cases:

$$[m, n, \varphi] = [\varphi, \varphi, \varphi] = \varphi$$

The following theorem can then be stated:

Given a triad of distinguishable components then a state which allows no distinguishable components to exist will result if either

(1) *any one component ceases to be distinguishable, or*
(2) *any pair of components become identical.*

We have previously given an example of this in the case of the triad:

[*inside, outside, boundary*]

where if the boundary is eliminated, also the inside and outside cease to exist as distinguishable entities. And also if the inside and outside become indistinguishable, then the boundary can no longer exist as an entity. In either case then the original state φ in which no distinguishable entities exist is re-established.

The theorem can also be stated in another form where its implication are clearer:

It is not possible for a single entity or a pair of entities to exist by itself or to be definable.

Now, this runs counter both to everyday assumptions and also to the assumptions on which traditional theories of logic and mathematics are based. We do normally assume that entities such as say a cup, table, window, human being can each exist and be individually defined as independent elements. If we now come to characteristics such as light then it is more easily seen that this exists relative to what is dark and similarly good is an attribute as distinguished from that which is evil. In fact however every distinguishable entity is demarcated and defined relative to what it is not. But even a dual pair is not sufficient to provide a basis for definition unless the distinction made is introduced as a third term, and in this case we come back to the triad as the minimal definitional unit for any form of entities.

7.7. Types of definitional units

According to the basic axiom the components of a triad are definable in terms of one another. Given the definition previously arrived at of a pair and of individual components, the definitional unit can be represented in the form:

$$\left.\begin{array}{l} m \, n = p \\ p \, n = m \\ p \, m = n \end{array}\right\} \text{definitional unit}$$

where each individual component is defined in terms of the remaining pair.

No other kind of definitional form is possible since if we set up a definition of the type $m = n$, then, as we have seen, the whole triad of components ceases to exist as distinguishable entities.

The point of departure was the triad of undefined components $[m, n, p]$. Since at this point the representation of a definitional unit has made use of the definition of pair formation, this definition (p. 91) has to explicitly form part of the triad which generates units of this type. The triad then takes the form:

[*m, n, pair formation*]

Pair formation as a defined term represents itself a definitional unit, and differs in this respect from the remaining components which will from here on be referred to as elements.

A definitional unit then consists of the three possible pairs *mm*, *nn* and *mn = nm* which define the two elements *m*, and *n*.

It is found that there are in this case not more than three possible types of definitional unit. These are shown in Table 7.1.

Table 7.1. Possible types of definitional unit.

| | Defines element | | | | | |
Pair	Type A 1	2	Type B 1	2	Type C 1	2
nn	n	m	n	n	m	m
mm	n	m	m	m	n	n
n m = m n	m	n	n	m	n	m

We are given that n and m are distinguishable elements, but neither has as yet any identifiable characteristics. The form of a definitional unit is therefore not changed if we exchange the labels n and m.

Thus given Type A in the form:

$$\left. \begin{array}{l} n\,n = n \\ m\,m = n \\ n\,m = m\,n = m \end{array} \right\} \quad \text{Type A (1)}$$

If in the above we exchange the letters n and m then we obtain Type A in the form:

$$\left.\begin{array}{r} m\,m = m \\ n\;n\; = m \\ m\,n = n\,m\; = n \end{array}\right\} \text{ Type A (2)}$$

The following are the characteristics of each type of definitional unit.

Type A distinguishes between pairs composed of identical elements (mm) and (nn) and pairs composed of different elements (mn) and (nm). If pairs of like elements are used to define the element n, then pairs of unlike elements define the element m.

The definitional unit can be shown to correspond to the second principle which applies to the Spencer-Brown cross operation, and corresponds in logic to 'negation of the statement P', in set theory to 'the complement of the set P', and in algebra to 'the inverse of P', or 'the dual of P'.

Type B. A pair of like elements defines the element included in the pair. That is $n\,n = n$ and $m\,m = m$ (for instance in algebra, $0 + 0 = 0$ and $1 \times 1 = 1$). Pairs of unlike elements can be used to define either n or m. However once a choice has been made then it is always possible for a dual independently definable unit of this type to exist.

This definitional unit can be shown to correspond to the first principle of Spencer-Brown's cross operation. In logic it corresponds to the dual pair:

P and Q
P or Q

where the statements P, Q can be either true or false. If one of these expressions is represented by the form Type B (1), than the other has the form of Type B (2). It should be noted however that transformation to the dual form requires that the concept of duality based on definitional unit Type A is given.

In set theory the Type B unit corresponds to the dual pair:

intersection of sets P and Q
union of sets P and Q

and in the algebra of Boolean rings the Type B unit corresponds to the dual pair:

multiplication of P and Q
addition of P and Q.

Type C. Pairs of like elements define the element not included in the pair. That is $n\ n = m$ and $m\ m = n$. Pairs of unlike elements can be used to define either m or n.

This definitional unit does not correspond to any of the expressions which have been used in developing the various basic forms of logic and mathematics. Sheffer (1913) introduced what he called the stroke operation $P \mid Q$ and went on to show that this single operational symbol is sufficient to express all the various forms of logical operations. This expression does in fact constitute a Type C definitional unit.

The cross operation has in sentential logic the corresponding form:

$$P \mid Q = \text{not } (P \text{ and } Q) \hspace{4cm} \text{Type C}$$

and therefore:

$$P \mid P = \text{not } (P \text{ and } P)$$

Then provided that we are given that:

$$P \text{ and } P = P \hspace{6cm} \text{Type B}$$

it follows that:

$$P \mid P = \text{not } P \hspace{6cm} \text{Type A.}$$

It has been claimed that Sheffer's stroke operation $P \mid Q$ is by itself sufficient to derive the field of logic. This however is seen not to be the case since the proof has to make use of the form $P \mid P$ which corresponds to 'negation of P and this is a Type A unit which has to be independently defined.

7.8. The axioms of logic and mathematics

We can now state as a theorem that:

The basic systems of logic and mathematics are derivable from any given pair of definitional units of Type A, B and C.

Type B and C can appear in two dual forms and any form can be chosen. Type A can appear in only one and thus self-dual form. There are eight possible pairs, any one of which provide a sufficient axiom set. These are AB_1, AB_2, AC_1, AC_2, B_1C_1, B_1C_2, B_2C_1 and B_2C_2.

The theorem is demonstrable within any of the basic types of logic and mathematics. Table 2 shows the pairs of axiomatic definitions which can be utilised. With the exception of Sheffer's form of logic, the pair of axiomatic principles chosen corresponds to definitional units Type A and B. The reason for this is that only the Type A and Type B definitional unit are expressible in terms of a single demonstrable operation.

This also applies to the two principles which were used by Spencer-Brown to generate the structure of logic. What becomes clear from Table 7.2, is that *each of the definitional units which have been derived correspond to an operation on a set of elements.*

Table 7.2. Showing that the axioms which generate the basic types of logic and mathematics correspond to a pair of definitional units.

Basic axioms of	Definitional unit		
	Type A	Type B	Type C
Sentential logic	Opposite of P	P or Q	
Set theory	Complement of P	Union of P and Q	
Algebra of Boolean rings	Inverse of P	Addition of P and Q	
Sheffer's stroke operation	$P \mid P$		$P \mid Q$
Spencer-Brown's cross operation	⫬	⫬⫬	

We have arrived at the end of the demonstration that given a triad of undefined elements which are definable in terms of one another, then this is sufficient to generate the logical structure in terms of which the world is apprehended. However, we are still at the stage where the components of the structures evolved are undefined elements. The next step is to investigate to what extent the definitional units make it possible to derive some of the basic system concepts which we utilize to identify specific characteristics of the phenomenal world.

In the following it will be shown that this becomes possible if we make use of an operational interpretation of the three types of definitional unit. To do so we need however to show that the concept of an operation is derivable from the basic axiom.

7.9. Operations, directionality and time

The triadic form which defines the concept of an operation is

[*preceeding state (S_n), subsequent state (S_m), operation π*]

so that if the operation π is applied to the state S_n what results is the state S_m. This can be put in the form of

$$\pi\,(S_n) \rightarrow S_m$$

We note that an operation generates a specific direction which takes us from one distinguishable form to another. Also an operation generates the concept of time, since it creates a distinction between a state which lies or was before and a state which lies or comes to be after. Any triadic form which has these characteristics of directionality will then have the characteristics of an operational unit.

It was shown to begin with how a primary distinction in the form of a boundary creates a triadic set [m, n, p]. Next it was found that if a further distinction in the form of a boundary is made within this set then we obtain pairs and individual elements as follows

$$[m, n, p] \quad \overset{\displaystyle \longrightarrow}{\underset{\displaystyle \longrightarrow}{\longrightarrow}} \quad \begin{array}{l} [(m\ n)\ p] \\ [(m\ p)\ n] \\ [(n\ \ p)\ m] \end{array}$$

What has been produced at this stage is an operational unit. Direction is uniquely defined, since in this way we can only go from the triad to sets of pairs and individuals. As a result what is generated is a preceeding and a subsequent state. The initial state is the triadic set, the operation is that of introducing a boundary within the triadic set, and the subsequent state are possible pairs and individual elements. The conceptual characteristics of an operation are thus derivable from the basic axiom.

We note that a directional property is found also within each definitional unit. For instance a Type A unit has the form

$$\begin{matrix} n & n & \searrow \\ m & m & \nearrow \end{matrix} n$$

$$\begin{matrix} n & m & \searrow \\ m & n & \nearrow \end{matrix} m$$

The characteristics of each element in the triad is in this form uniquely defined consistent with the basic axiom. A definition of the form $nn = n$ can in this case be interpreted as an operation on an initial state which leads to a subsequent state as an outcome.

7.10. Types of Operational Systems

Up to this stage, the elements n and m of the basic triad have remained without definable characteristics. We shall now show that each of the definitional units constitutes an operational system, and that within each system the elements aquire specifiable characteristics. This is not the case however for the Type C unit, which accounts for the fact that this unit has not normally been made use of in the development of logic or in the construction of scientific theories.

Type A system

The type A definitional unit can be put in the form of a table below

	n	m
n	n	m
m	m	n

The properties of this operational system become more clearly visible if this is put in form of a diagram (Figure 7.4).

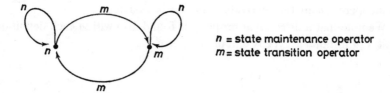

n = state maintenance operator
m = state transition operator

Fig. 7.4. State transition diagram for operational system. Type A.

If we start of with element *n* and apply *n*, then we come back again to the element *n*. As long as we do this, the element *n*, will be produced over and over again, until the element *m* is applied, and as soon as this happens, a transition will occur to the element *m*. If we now apply *n*, then as often as we do this the element *m* is reconstituted. However, if we again apply *m*, then a transition to element *n* occurs. Since the elements *n* and *m* can be interchanged without affecting the properties of the system, *n* and *m* constitute *dual elements*.

Inspection of the diagram makes it clear that:

  n is a *state maintenance operator.*

To whatever element this operator is applied, this maintains the element in existence.

  m is a *state transition operator.*

To whatever element this operator is applied, the element ceases to exist and the dual element is created. If we continue to apply this operator what results is an oscillation between the two elements, similar to what happens in an alternating current, or in figure – ground reversal.

If we denote the two elements by 0 and 1, the repeated application of the state maintenance operator leads to sequences

  1, 1, 1, 1, 1, . . . *or* 0, 0, 0, 0, 0, . . .

where a form is maintained.

Repeated application of the state transition operator leads to the sequence

  1, 0, 1, 0, 1, 0, 1 . . .

Each of these processes can be found in both material and behaviour systems.

Matter and Waves

The Type A system restricted to repetitive sequences of the state maintenance and state transition operation generates the basic attributes in terms of which we apprehend the material world. The material world is apprehended by us either in the way of form maintaining objects, that is entities which are perceived as maintaining an identical form, or in the form of wave like oscillating phenomena. What we classify as constituting the physical world are those phenomena, which are apprehended as matter, that is identity maintaining entities or as wave phenomena. Restricted to these two possibilities, matter and waves constitute dual forms in terms of which the structure of the physical world comes to be apprehended.

The process generated by the two operations is shown in Figure 7.5.

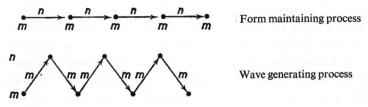

Form maintaining process

Wave generating process

Figure 7.5.

We tend to perceive objects which retain their form as having static characteristics, while processes of change are easily recognized as constituting dynamic processes. However, it will be seen at this stage that also identity maintenance of objects, which we conceive to be located in our environment, is a continuous and dynamic process in which throughout our waking life we are ceaselessly involved.

The two dynamic processes which generate waves and identity maintaining forms are similar in their structural form. A wave form is a process moving continuously between alternative states. A material form can be looked at as a special case of such a wave form which as, a process, is continuously restricted to a single state. The form in which we have discovered the identity and form maintaining process is shown in Figure 7.6.

Fig. 7.6. Form maintenance
as a cyclic process.

This can be looked at as a wave which is so to say locked into itself. That is, a continuously cyclic process which revolves around itself, until it is disrupted, when the form disappears and it then turns into a wavelike oscillating process until it is again bound into an identity maintaining form.

During the intermediate period when no stable identification is possible we are faced with a situation of uncertainty which is essentially one of oscillation between alternatives, until the process again becomes locked into a single form, and uncertainty is removed.

We are familiar with representations of this type for matter at the atomic level. The derivation however shows that the same type of process is involved in the generation of all kinds of identity maintaining forms. That is, the generation of the ordinary objects around us in so far as these appear to be unchanging, and of those permanent characteristics which we attribute to persons and organizations. And also we ourselves, in so far as we seek to maintain a stable identity, constitute ourselves as a continuously repetitive self-enclosed and self-maintaining process which, when it becomes disrupted leads to a state of uncertainty which may be experienced as intolerable. It is possible also to remain in this state of uncertainty for some time unable or unwilling to lock oneself into a self-repetitive form. It is to the extent that behavior is restricted to these two types of processes (which however it does not need to be) that its structure becomes analogous to the structure of material entities. This is the case since the process which generates the perception of identity maintaining objects in the environment, generates in the same way the enduring and permanent characteristics which we attribute to ourselves to other persons and to social organizations.

The dynamic system which has been discussed is generated by a statement of the type 'take the opposite or the inverse of an element P.' We are here able to confirm Piaget's theory that identity maintenance depends on an operational system which has the property of reversibility.

Type B system

The Type B definitional unit can be put in the form of a table below:

	n	m
n	n	m
m	m	m

Given the element n and applying n we arrive back at n. In every other case we arrive at m. The diagram showing the operational system which is generated is shown in Figure 7.7.

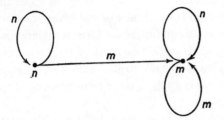

Fig. 7.7. State transition diagram for operational system. Type B.

n is as before as an identity maintaining operator. Starting with state n, if n is applied, then the state n is maintained in existence. Starting with state m, if n is applied, then state m is maintained in existence. m is a *displacement operator*. A state transition occurs only however if this operator is applied to the state n, but not if it is applied to the state m.

While the basic characteristic of the Type A system is that its processes are reversible, the basic characteristic of the Type B system is that its processes are *irreversible*. Once we have left state n, there is no way in which we can come back to it again, and once we arrived at state m, there is no way in which we can come out of it again.

The Type B system is separable into two distinct process structures as shown in Figure 7.8.

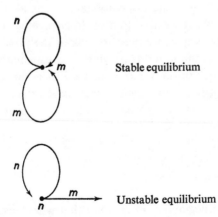

Stable equilibrium

Unstable equilibrium

Figure 7.8.

Just as previously, identity maintaining entities and waves were found to be generated as dual forms, so here in the same way stable and unstable equilibrium states are generated as dual forms in terms of which the dynamic characteristics of the environment and also of ourselves come to be apprehended.

In the case of unstable equilibrium, a form is maintained in existence until an operation is applied which leads out of the form which then ceases to exist, and there is no way back to it. In the case of stable equilibrium no matter what operation is applied, there is no way out of the state once it has come into existence.

An example might be a stone on a hill top which stays there until it is displaced. Once this happens it rolls down until it comes to rest on a limitless plain. Once there, whether it stays in the same spot or is displaced, there is nowhere else it can move.

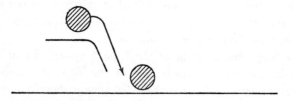

Fig. 7.9. Illustrating the transition from unstable to stable equilibrium.

The two definitional units thus not only generate the basic types of logic and mathematics, but apparently also the basic concepts sufficient for building a theory of physics.

If we wish to show how these operational systems also generate a psychological theory then what we need to do is to change our perspective. Instead of attending to the output, we need to look at the process which generates the conceptual structure in terms of which the apparently objective characteristics of the environment are apprehended. It is the same process which as consequences of the initial distinction between the self and the environment generates and constitutes what we take to be the enduring structure of ourselves.

Re-view

Going back to the beginning we now see that what was called the original state is not originally the original state but only becomes this *after* a primary distinction has been made. And also this state which was said to be void of characteristics and thus undefinable is in fact defined relative to the state in which definable elements exist.

What we now find is that the *primary distinction between self and environment does not create a single triad but a triad of triads* as shown in Figure 7.10.

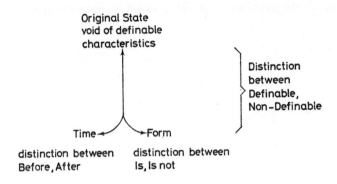

Figure 7.10.

A primary distinction having been made, the state void of characteristics conceived of as a distinct and separate object is generated *together* with the state in which definable elements exist. And thus, a world in which definable characteristics exist is not, to begin with, created from a *prior* state void of characteristics.

When to begin with we conceived of a state void of characteristics which became subject to a primary distinction resulting in a world of definable elements, then the primary distinction had already been made, and the state void of characteristics which is apprehended at this stage is only one of relative void.

As long as we are concerned with before and after, the existing and the non-existing, the non-definable as opposed to the definable, then we are in the realm of the primary distinction. And also if we conceive of something outside this realm, then we are still within the realm of the primary distinction.

The primary distinction of inside, boundary and outside constitutes the identification of the inside with its boundary as a self and of the outside as the environment. The maintenance of the primary distinction is the maintenance of a self as a distinguishable and enduring entity perceiving itself as confronting the environment as an object.

When a triadic set of elements is generated, then characteristics of each of the elements such as inside, boundary and outside become manifest in their mutual dependence on one another.

Apart from a triadic definitional unit and by itself, there are no elements with distinguishable characteristics. And so, that which manifests itself as elements with specific characteristics within a triadic set, is and remains in its nature not different from that which is void of characteristics.

Epilogue

8. Types of social research

Research relationship	Product	General type of research
Researcher-object	*The product is a theory.* The data and those from whom the data are obtained are looked at as dispensible after use. The theory is assumed to retain eternal validity.	Basic research
Researcher-client	*The product is a new system.* The theory is given in advance and does not basically change as a result of research.	Applied research
Collaborative researcher-organization relationship. Research capacity is gradually built into the organization as a necessary condition for a self-maintaining learning process	*The product is a new process.* 1. The theory about the existing organization will no longer be relevant after the new type of organization has been established. 2. The new organization is a point of departure for exploring further developmental possibilities (Figure 8.1).	Action research

Fig. 8.1. Phases in action research contain basic and applied research as part components in a different form and context.

Literature

Blichfeldt, J. F. et al.: *To forforsøk med åpne undervisningsoppgaver* (Two preliminary experiments with open learning tasks), Work Research Inst. Doc. 21., Oslo, 1973.

Blichfeldt, J. F.: *Organizational Change as the Development of Networks and Mutual Trust*, Work Research Inst. Doc. 23., Oslo, 1973.

Blichfeldt, J. F.: *Skole møter skole* (School meets School), Tanum, Oslo, 1975.

Boole, G.: *An Investigation of the Laws of Thought*, Cambridge, 1854.

Chardin, T. de: *The Phenomenon of Man*, Harper, New York, 1959.

Dewey, J.: *The Quest for Certainty: A Study of the Relation of Knowledge and Action*, (Gifford Lectures) New York, 1929.

Emery, F. E., Oeser, O. A. and Tully, J.: *Information, Decision and Action*, Melbourne University Press, Melbourne, 1958.

Emery, F. E.: Democratization of the Work Place, *Manpower and Applied Psychology*, 1967, 1, 3.

Emery, F. E.: The Next Thirty Years, *Human Relations*, 1967, 20, 3.

Emery, F. E.: *Futures We're In*. Center for Continuing Education, A.N.U., Canberra, 1974.

Emery, F. E. and Emery, M.: *Participative Design*, Center for Continuing Education, A.N.U., Canberra, 1974.

Emery, F. E. and Thorsrud, E.: *Democracy at Work*, Martinus Nijhoff, Social siences Division, Leiden, 1976.

Engelstad, P. H.: *Teknologi og social forandring på arbeidsplassen* (Technology and Social Change in the Work Place). Tanum, Oslo, 1970.

Engelstad, P. H.: Socio-Technical Approach to Problems of Process Control, in Davis, E. L. & Taylor, J. C.: *Design of Jobs*, Penguin, Harmondsworth, 1972.

Festinger, L.: *A Theory of Cognitive Dissonance*, Row, Peterson, 1957.

Gulowsen, J.: *Selvstyrte arbeidsgrupper* (Autonomous Work Groups), Tanum, Oslo, 1971.

Gulowsen, J.: A Measure of Work-Group Autonomy, in Davis, E. L. & Taylor, J. C.: *Design of Jobs*, Penguin, Hammondsworth, 1972.

Heider, F.: Attitudes and Cognitive Organization *J. Psychol.*, 1946, 21, 107-112.

Herbst, P. G.: *Autonomous Group Functioning*, Tavistock Publ., London, 1962.

Herbst, P. G.: *Behavioural Worlds*, Tavistock Publ., London, 1970.

Herbst, P. G.: *Socio-Technical Design*, Tavistock Publ., London, 1974.

Herbst, P. G.: *Two Visits to 'Volvo' Kalmar*, Work Research Inst. Doc. 7. (Restricted), Oslo, 1975.

Hill, P.: *Towards a New Philosophy of Management*, Gower Press, Epping, 1971.

Hobbes, T.: *Leviathan*, London, 1651.

Kingdon, R. D.: *Matrix Organization: Managing Information Technologies*, Tavistock Publ., London,1973.

Lie, S. S.: Regulated Social Change: A Diffusion Study of the Norwegian Comprehensive School Reform, *Acta Sociologica*, 1973, 16, 4, 332-352.

Mao Tse Tung: On Contradiction, (1937), in *Essential Works of Chinese Communism*, Chai, W. (Ed) Bantam N.Y. (1969).

Meadows, D. H.: *Limits to Growth*, Earth Island Ltd., London, 1972.

Newcomb, T. M.: An Approach to the Study of Communicative Acts, *Psych. Rev.*, 1953, 60, 393-404.

Pascal, B.: *Pensées*, (1670), Editions du Seuil, Paris, (1962).

Pattersen, E. M. and Rutherford, D. E.: *Elementary Abstract Algebra*, Oliver & Boyd, London, 1965.

Peirce, C. S.: *Collected Papers*, Cambridge, Mass., 1933.

Pepper, S. C.: *World Hypotheses*, Univ. of California Press, Berkeley, 1961.

Piaget, J.: *Logic and Psychology*, Manchester Univ. Press, Manchester, 1953.

Qvale, T. U.: *Job Redesign in the U.K.*, Work Research Inst. Doc. 46., Oslo, 1973.

Rice, K.: *Productivity and Social Organization: The Ahmedabad Experiment*, Tavistock Publ., London, 1958.

Rochin, R. I.: The Subsistence Farmer as Innovator: A Field Survey, *South Asian Review*, 1973, 6, 4, 280-302.

Roggema, J. and Thorsrud, E.: *Et skip i utvikling* (A Developmental Ship), Tanum, Oslo, 1974.

Roggema, J. and Hammarstrøm, N. K.: *Nye organisasjonsformer til sjøs* (New Forms of Organization at Sea), Tanum, Oslo, 1975.

Rogne, K.: Redesigning the Process of Superstructure Design, *Applied Ergonomics*, 1974, 5, 4, 213-218.

Sheffer, H. M.: *Trans. Amer. Math. Soc.*, 1913, 14, 481-8.

Sommerhoff, G.: *Analytical Biology*, Oxford University Press, London, 1950.

Spencer-Brown, L.: *Laws of Form*, Allen and Unwin, London, 1969.

Thorsrud, E.: A Strategy for Research and Social Change in Industry, *Social Science Information* 1970, 9, 5.

Thorsrud, E.: Policy Making as a Learning Process, in Cherns A.B., *et al.* (Eds.): *Social Science and Government Policies and Problems*, Tavistock Publ., London, 1972.

Thorsrud, E.: Democratization of Work as a Process of Change Towards Non-Bureaucratic Types of Organization, in Hofstede, G. and Kassem, M. S. (Eds.): *European Contributions to Organization Theory*, Van Gorcum, Assen 1976.

Trist, E. L. and Bamforth, K. W.: Some Social and Psychological Consequences of the Longwall Method of Goal-getting, *Human Relations*, 1951, 4, 3-38.

Trist, E. L., *et al.*: *Organizational Choice: The Loss, Re-discovery and Transformation of a Work Tradition*, Tavistock Publ., London, 1963.

Trist, E. L.: The Professional Facilitation of Planned Change in Organizations, *Proceedings 16th International Congress of Applied Psychology*, Swets and Zaitlinger, Amsterdam, 1968.

Walton, R. E.: *Organizational Innovation – Half Life and After life*, Harvard Business School, Graduate School of Business Administration, Doc. 13, Cambridge, Mass., 1973.

Waley, A.: *Three Ways of Thought in Ancient China*. Doubleday, New York, 1939.